Tips and Traps
for New
Home
Owners

Other McGraw-Hill Books by Robert Irwin

Tips and Traps When Buying a Home

Tips and Traps When Selling a Home

*Tips and Traps When Buying a Co-Op, Condo,
  or Townhouse*

Tips and Traps for Making Money in Real Estate

Tips and Traps When Renovating Your Home

How to Find Hidden Real Estate Bargains

How to Buy a Home When You Can't Afford It

How to Get Started in Real Estate Investing

Home Buyer's Checklist

Home Seller's Checklist

Home Renovation Checklist

Home Closing Checklist

Buy, Rent, and Sell

Tips and Traps
for New
Home
Owners

Robert Irwin

McGraw-Hill

New York Chicago San Francisco Lisbon London
Madrid Mexico City Milan New Delhi San Juan
Seoul Singapore Sydney Toronto

1 2 3 4 5 6 7 8 9 0 FGR/FGR 0 1 0 9 8 7 6 5 4

ISBN 0-07-144542-0

This publication is designed to provide accurate and authoritative information in regard to the subject matter covered. It is sold with the understanding that neither the author nor the publisher is engaged in rendering legal, accounting, or other professional service. If legal advice or other expert assistance is required, the services of a competent professional person should be sought.

> —*From a Declaration of Principles jointly adopted by Committee of the American Bar Association and a Committee of Publishers.*

McGraw-Hill books are available at special quantity discounts to use as premiums and sales promotions, or for use in corporate training programs. For more information, please write to the Director of Special Sales, McGraw-Hill Professional, Two Penn Plaza, New York, NY 10121-2298. Or contact your local bookstore.

 This book is printed on recycled, acid-free paper containing a minimum of 50% recycled, de-inked fiber.

Contents

Preface   vii

Part 1 Get Your Home Finances in Order   1

1. How Much is Enough Insurance?   3

2. When Should You Refinance?   21

3. Can You Really Improve Your Home's Value through Renovation?   33

4. Watching Out for Value Grabbers   51

5. Record Keeping and Tax Deductions for Homeowners   61

6. Tax Planning for When You Sell   77

7. Security for Your Home   85

8. Did You Pay Too Much?   101

Part 2 A Home Operating Manual   121

9. The *Before* You Move in Checklist   123

10. Surviving the Move   131

11. Upgrading Your Home   137

12. Your Home Maintenance Schedule   181

Appendix: Tips When Renovating Your Home   193

Index   201

Preface

When you buy a car, you get an owner's manual. When you buy a television set, the first things on top of the box are the instructions. Even when you buy a can opener, a little piece of paper usually comes along telling you how to use it.

That's why when my editor at McGraw-Hill, Mary Glenn, first suggested a Tips and Traps book for new home owners, my reaction was— of course! Why not an instruction manual when you get your new home? What could be more obvious? Or more needed?

I've needed it myself. With my family, I've personally moved eight times over the last few decades (including moves to both existing and new homes and one that we built from the ground up). Each time the move was a major effort, and each time I wished I had a list of things to do, to expect, and to understand about the new home.

Well, after eight moves, you can imagine that I've accumulated enough memories and wisdom to get pretty good at it. Besides, I've talked with hundreds of people who have moved as part of buying and selling real estate. So I've put down what I think are the important things that every new home owner should know, along with a fair amount of relevant information on real estate and home ownership.

The book is divided into two sections. In the first are all the financial considerations, from insurance to pricing for the eventual resale. The second section is devoted to checklists and suggestions for upgrading your home.

I wish I'd had this little book each time that I moved. I hope that it will prove immensely useful to you in your new home.

Tips and Traps for New Home Owners

Part 1

Get Your Home Finances in Order

1
How Much Is Enough Insurance?

By the time you move into your new home, you will already have it insured. This is not because you had great foresight and put a policy on your property in advance of escrow closing. It's simply because no lender will issue a mortgage unless you carry enough insurance to cover it in the event of a fire or other catastrophe.

Thus, the insurance that most of us begin with doesn't so much insure us, as it insures the lender. For many people, concerns about insurance end there... until there's a claim. However, the smart new home owner will examine the property and his or her need for insurance and make appropriate adjustments. You might need to add new insurance, to change the policy to save money on the premium, or simply to leave things as they are. However, just overlooking your insurance needs and leaving things to chance risks possibly losing your home and/or your possessions!

Why Do We Need Insurance, Anyway?

We don't, as long as nothing bad happens to us. If we never get sick, we don't need health insurance. If we live to a ripe old age, we don't need life insurance. And if our house never burns down, we don't need fire insurance.

The trouble is, we don't know. We can never know what the future will bring. Thus, to reduce our exposure to financial loss because of some unexpected disaster, most responsible people carry some insurance.

The two big questions are:

- What should I insure?
- How much insurance should I carry?

NOTE: The purpose of this chapter is to present an overview of the typical kinds of insurance a homeowner might need or want. The author is not engaged in selling insurance. If you want or need insurance, check with a professional.

Are You Overinsured?

When starting out in a new home, you can easily get overinsured. The best example of this comes from the many appliances that new home owners buy. (Major home retailers like Lowe's and Home Depot calculate that the new home owner will spend something like $10,000 on new appliances and home improvement projects in the first six months of home ownership.)

When you buy any home appliance from a refrigerator to a dishwasher to a computer (I include computers in this list because they have become a staple in most homes today), you are almost always offered the opportunity to buy insurance to cover the new item. That way, if the new appliance breaks, the insurance will pay to have it fixed. If it can't be fixed, the insurance will have it replaced, often with no questions asked.

Sound good? It's not a bad plan—except for the cost. The problem is that typically this type of individual appliance insurance is very expensive, often 20 percent or more of the original cost of the appliance per year. Further, it might be completely unnecessary.

Consider Table 1.1, which shows a list of items you might purchase that can be insured:

To insure all of these appliances individually, it can easily cost you $1300 annually. And because most policies ask you for two to three years of insurance up front, that's $2600 to $5200 you must initially come up with.

So what's the problem?

The trouble is that you might not need the insurance. First off, all of these items come with some sort of warranty, typically a minimum of 90 days and sometimes with one-year full parts and labor warranties.

Table 1.1 Typical Home Appliances That Might Be Insured

	Cost	Annual Insurance cost (@20%)
Refrigerator	$1,000	$200
Freezer	900	180
Stove	500	100
Dish Washer	500	100
TV	600	120
Entertainment Center	1,500	300
Vacuum cleaner	200	40
Lawn mower	300	60
Computer	1,000	200
	6,500	1,300

Further, for most appliances you can buy these days, particularly if they're electronic, if they're going to burn out, they will often do so within the first three weeks of operation. On the other hand, if they don't immediately crash, chances are that they will keep on running for years.

TIP—LOOK FOR HOME WARRANTY PLANS

You might already have insurance to cover some of your home appliances. In most home purchases, the seller pays for a "home warranty" plan. This typically insures you, the buyer, for one year against breakage of your home appliances and systems (such as heating, air conditioning, water heater, dishwasher and so on, but not usually including computer or home entertainment centers). If a covered item breaks, you call a designated repair service and pay a deductible, usually under $50, to get it repaired. (If it can't be repaired, you are usually given an allowance toward a new appliance.) After one year, you often are given the option of extending the plan for an additional year or more. In an older house where older items are likely to break down, it might be a bargain, provided the insurer doesn't jack the premium up too high. In a new home, you might want to take your chances without this additional insurance.

Second, the cost of the insurance by individually covering each appliance is astronomical. If your premiums run around 20 percent of the cost, as indicated here, you might be better off self-insuring. In our example, the $1300 annually spent on appliance insurance might be better put into an interest-earning account. Assuming nothing breaks, at the end of five years the account would have $6500+, which could then be used to buy a bunch of brand new appliances. And if something does break, there would be that account ready to take care of it. (Vendors are well aware of all of this and that's why the commission paid to salespeople on appliance insurance is often higher than the commission on selling the appliance itself!)

Finally, many people drop their appliance insurance after five years (figuring the item is too old and obsolete to spend all that money insuring it), just when it's entering the phase when it might, indeed, fail. Thus, assuming nothing actually breaks, you've paid for the appliance twice—once when you bought it and a second time when you insured it!

TRAP—SOME
HOME APPLIANCES
DO BREAK

There's the rub, and the rationale that vendors use to get you take the insurance. You can never know if and when an appliance will break. If they break, or get damaged (and the insurance covers it), then it's a bargain.

However, to my way of thinking you must assess the potential risks.

- What are the chances of appliances going out?
- Do I have other insurance to cover many of them (home warranty plan)?

■ Have I set aside a reserve fund to cover the cost of fixing or replacing appliances?

When all is said and done, I usually don't buy the appliance insurance. Of course, you'll have to make up your own mind. Just be careful not to be overinsured.

Are You Underinsured?

If you were recently a tenant, you might have been underinsured and never even known about it.

As a tenant living in a rented apartment, many people assume that if the building burns down (or is otherwise destroyed) and their personal property is destroyed with it, the landlord's insurance will cover them. Lose your furniture, your clothing, your computer and the landlord will cover your loss.

Nothing could be further from the truth. Assuming there wasn't negligence, the landlord often has no responsibility for a tenant's possessions. Rather, it's up to the tenant to carry personal property insurance often called "tenant's insurance." Carry that insurance and you're covered in a fire loss. Don't carry it and you lose it all. Because many tenants don't carry personal property insurance, either purposely or unwittingly, they are underinsured.

As soon as you move into your new home, you might also be underinsured. For example, when buying a fire-insurance policy, the insurance company will sometimes consult with you as to how much coverage you want. No, they won't ask directly. Instead, they might say something such as, "You've got 2000 square feet and according to our tables, in the event of a fire, it will cost $100 a square foot to replace the property if it's average construction, $125 if it's better grade construction, and $150 if it's custom. Our assessment is that your home falls somewhere between average and above-average so we can insure it for either $100 or $125 a square foot. Assuming the lower replacement cost satisfies your lender, which would you prefer?"

Most new home owners jump at the additional coverage, until they find out the premium. (The difference in premiums might be hundreds of dollars.) Then they often opt for the lower coverage. After all, what's the chance of the place burning down to the ground?

Unfortunately, it does happen. And, if you don't have enough coverage, you might not be able to rebuild your home. That's a case of being underinsured.

TRAP—NOT KEEPING
UP WITH COSTS

Most insurers increase the amount of your coverage annually to keep up with the rising costs of construction. But not all insurers do this, or increase the amount enough. For example, when you buy, the replacement costs might be $100 a square foot. Five years later, with skyrocketing construction costs, they could be at $150 a square foot. You replacement insurance, however, might only have increased to $120 a square foot. You would be underinsured.

Set Aside an Insurance Day

When you're the owner of a home, you don't want to be overinsured—or underinsured. You want just the right amount of insurance to cover your needs.

This is why I suggest every homeowner set aside one day a year to look at and reconsider insurance needs. It can be on your birthday, April 15th (although if you owe taxes, that's a tough day to worry about insurance!), January 1st or whatever. On that day you'll look at all of the insurance coverage on your home and, along with a good insurance agent, decide if it's just right, if you don't have enough, or if you have too much.

TIP—EVERYONE'S
INSURANCE NEEDS
ARE DIFFERENT

Be sure you check with a good agent before decreasing or increasing any insurance coverage. This discussion is only intended to give you a general overview of property insurance.

When you check out your home insurance, here's what you're likely to consider:

Insurance Against Loss of the Property

One of your primary concerns should be to insure against the loss of your property. Your property consists of three distinct areas:

- Title
- Building
- Personal property

Title Insurance

Title to the land is insured through a policy of insurance that, presumably, you obtained from a title insurance company as part of your purchase.

TRAP—DID YOU GET TITLE INSURANCE?

Title insurance covering owners is not mandatory—title insurance covering the amount of the mortgage is necessary to get financing. Be sure that your title insurance not only covers the lender, but you as well.

Title insurance, unlike other types, works backward. It insures you against defects in the title that occurred before you made your purchase. For example, if a signature from a seller two owners before you was forged, presumably the title insurance would cover you against loss of your investment. For this reason you should be sure to get title insurance that covers the full amount you paid, including your down payment, not just the amount of your mortgage.

TIP—FIND OUT
WHAT'S COVERED

If you're not sure what your title insurance covers, go back to the title company that issued it and ask. It might be that you're covered only up to the value of the financing. You might want to increase the insurance to the full amount of the property's value. Of course, this was best done before escrow closed, but it usually can be handled shortly afterward.

Building and Personal Property Insurance

This usually has two options: There's a basic fire insurance policy that covers you against fires and a few other losses. Then there's the greater coverage of a homeowner's plan. This includes far more coverage against many more items.

Both of these plans usually cover your personal property as well. It's just that there's greater coverage under the homeowner's policy. Further, most homeowner's policies also cover you for liability, that is in case you are sued by someone who might, for example, fall over a bicycle located on your property and injure themselves.

Whenever possible, I suggest that you opt for the greater coverage of a homeowner's policy. The price is not usually that much higher (perhaps $750 when a basic policy might cost $500 annually), yet the coverage is extraordinarily better.

Of course, in some areas it might not be possible to get any conventional homeowner or fire insurance policy at all. This is typically in areas where there are great risks. In these cases there is usually a state organization that will create an "assigned risk" policy. (Sometimes it's directly available from insurers.) Here, all insurance companies who wish to do business in the state must agree to accept a certain number of these high-risk policies. Typically the premium is slightly higher, although in some cases only basic fire insurance— no homeowner's policy, is available.

If you try to buy a home in one of these areas and need financing, chances are you were directed to get an assigned risk policy. On the other hand, if you're already living in an area that becomes designated a high fire risk (usually because a fire swept through the area), you might find that suddenly your existing fire/homeowner's insurance is canceled and you can't find other insurance through the normal insurance agent channels!

Don't panic. Though it might take some time, there's usually a state agency willing to help.

**TRAP—CANCELED
FIRE INSURANCE CAN
THREATEN YOUR
MORTGAGE**

Your mortgage requires you to carry a minimum amount of fire insurance. If your policy is canceled, typically the lender will automatically put a minimum policy on your property and charge the premium to you. Don't rejoice, however. This policy only covers the amount of the mortgage and is usually quite expensive. You'll want to replace it with a better and less expensive policy of your own as soon as possible.

Disaster Insurance

While a homeowner's policy covers you against a great many risks, typically it will leave out the coverage that you most need! For example, in California, these policies usually do not cover you against earthquake damage. In the Midwest they typically do not cover against flooding. On parts of the East Coast they might not cover against hurricanes.

Rather, in order to get coverage against these risks, you will have to pay a higher premium, if insurers will even accept the coverage. In earthquake-prone areas, for example, insurers will not issue any insurance because they've learned through bitter experience that their chances of loss are too great.

However, once again, the state might come to the rescue. Some states, such as California with its self-insured earthquake plan, will offer you insurance. However, the premium cost is usually very high, the deductibles might be 10 or 20 percent, and the total coverage might be low. In order words, though some coverage might be available, it might be minimal.

TIP—FEDERAL BAILOUTS

Many homeowners do not buy this high-risk insurance and instead rely on the federal government to bail them out after a disaster. FEMA (Federal Emergency Management Agency) typically comes in after an earthquake, flood, or other similar natural disaster and offers low-interest loans, no-interest loans, or outright grants to help homeowners rebuild. While this might indeed happen, there are no guarantees.

Liability Limits

As noted earlier, most homeowner insurance plans offer some type of personal liability coverage. This can be far more extensive than you might imagine. For example, a neighbor's child might fall off a swing in your yard. Your plan probably will cover your liability.

However, in my case, my son and a friend were playing with a BB gun at the friend's house and the other child was accidentally shot in the face. Although neither family had approved of this play, and though the boy's injury was not severe, there were medical costs (paid for out of the medical payments section of the insurance) and a threatened lawsuit. However, because the boys had begun playing at my house before walking over to the friend's house, because it was accidental, and because the play was not condoned, my home-owner's insurance covered all costs.

This is not to say that your insurance plan will do the same, but it is comforting to know that you probably do have significant coverage around the home.

Running a Business from Home

There might, however, be exclusions. If you operate a business out of your home, your homeowner's plan might not offer you liability coverage. Coverage, however, might be extended IF you pay an additional premium.

This type of insurance is certainly needed as, for example, when owners run day care centers from their home. It's also necessary when any other business activity is run out of the home from teaching piano lessons to operating an accounting firm. Anytime you have a business where people walk into your home, you'll need to have good liability coverage. (You never know when they might trip, fall, and injure themselves.)

Special Liability for Pools and Spas

If you have a pool or a spa, you will want to carry very high liability insurance, typically in the range of a million dollars or more. These are two areas where the risk of accidents is very high. If someone is injured, or God forbid, drowns in your pool or spa, a lawsuit is almost automatic.

I wouldn't have a pool or spa with liability insurance of less than a million dollars. However, you will find that your homeowner's insurance policy limits the maximum exposure of the insurer, typically to around $100,000. Sometimes you can increase this maximum to up to $300,000, but after that getting additional coverage through your homeowner's plan might be difficult.

TIP—LOOK FOR AN UMBRELLA PLAN

Many (but not all) insurers offer "umbrella" plans. This is a separate liability policy over and above your homeowner's that begins coverage where your homeowner's ends and goes up to several millions of dollars. For example, it might start at $100,000 (if that's the limit of your homeowner's plan) and go to $2,000,000. The cost is usually minimal, perhaps $500 hundred dollars a year. It's a real bargain when you need high liability coverage. However, the insurer might only offer it if you buy all your insurance from it, both home and auto. Sometimes it can be worth changing insurers to find one who offers an umbrella plan—I did.

Covering Special Needs

While a homeowner's plan might cover most of your insurance requirements, you might have special needs. For example, perhaps you have a number of furs, or rare paintings, or fine jewelry, or rare coins. You want these covered in case of fire or theft.

Most homeowner plans will cover these automatically, but to a low amount. For example, they might be covered to a maximum of $1000 for each incident. If, however, you value your paintings at $25,000, you would be severely underinsured.

However, as is often the case, for an additional premium, you might be able to increase the coverage for these items. Typically called "floaters," you might be required to list items covered and provide appraisals in order to get coverage. However, if your needs for coverage are very high, say $100,000 or a million dollars, you will probably need to get a special plan in addition to your home-owner's. Ask your insurance agent to direct you to those who specialize in these.

Tricks of Homeowner's Insurance

There's the old joke about how most homeowner's insurance covers you against a stampede by a herd of wild elephants. If you ask the agent about this, you might be told, "See how good the insurance is—we've never had to pay a claim!"

The contrary side is that you might not be insured against something that you badly need coverage for. The most recent notorious example of this is black mold.

The Terror of Black Mold

Black mold is a fungus that occurs in most homes. It is associated with moisture and typically occurs around bathrooms, washrooms, and kitchens, though it can occur in wet basements, attics, or walls. It's been around as long as anyone can remember.

Recently, however, there has been an almost hysterical fear of "killer" black mold. This is, apparently, a type of black mold that may be able to cause serious allergies, illness, or even death.

I don't know whether or not such a mold commonly exists. And as of this writing, the CDC (Center for Disease Control) has not issued a definitive statement about it. However, whether or not it's for real, people fear it. Some have insisted that insurance companies do extensive and expensive work removing it from homes. Perhaps you've seen crews in bubble suits removing black mold from the walls, ceilings, and floors of affected houses.

When insurance companies began rejecting claims, owners—particularly in Florida and Texas—sued them and won a string of expensive lawsuits. Indeed, right now black mold is probably the most contentious area between buyers and sellers of homes. Many buyers simply refuse to purchase unless the sellers guarantee that all black mold has been removed. Many sellers refuse to deal with such buyers because of the costs of removal.

From an insurance perspective, the costs of removing black mold have hit insurance companies hard. Therefore, most insurers now exclude some or all black mold coverage. While in the past black mold was commonly covered under water damage, today if you call your insurer to make a claim, you might find it's excluded under your policy. Or that coverage is for a low limit. Indeed, you might find that getting coverage against black mold is no longer possible. If you find it in your home, you might be on your own.

Cancellations, Nonrenewals, Premium Increases

Further, if you make a claim for black mold (or any water-related damage) to your insurer, you could find that your policy is later cancelled (if the insurer has reserved the right), nonrenewed, or your premium is increased. This is another little trick that insurers are playing.

Most of us are aware that making repeated claims against our *auto* insurance can result in higher premiums, or worse, cancellation or nonrenewal of our auto policy. That's why with so many small fender-benders, the party that causes the accident will offer to pay cash for the other party's repairs, rather than report it to the insurance company. In the long run, it can be cheaper for you to have the other car fixed than to have your insurance take care of it, particularly for fender-benders.

In the past that was not the case with homeowner's insurance. You could make as many legitimate claims as you needed, without fear of some sort of reprisal. Apparently, that's no longer the case.

According to owners and agents to whom I've talked, making several claims on your homeowner's insurance can cause your premiums to rise. Further, making certain types of claims, such as for black mold, or for water damage (which can lead to black mold down the road), might cause your insurer to consider canceling or not renewing your policy. (And if that happens, you might find it difficult to get homeowner's insurance from other companies.)

Of course, this is on a case-by-case basis. If you have a legitimate claim, then you should be entitled to claim it—that's why you buy insurance in the first place! You should discuss the filing of claims, and possible repercussions, with your agent. Your insurer might be far more liberal... or conservative in its approach to claims.

Playing with Deductibles

Typically you can choose from a variety of deductibles for your homeowner's policy. These range from as little as $50 per incident, to $1000 and higher. The deductible is the portion you pay when you have a claim.

In these days of rapidly rising premiums, it usually makes good sense to keep as high a deductible as possible. To illustrate why, here's what happened to me.

I used to have a $100 deductible policy. In case I had a claim, I would pay the first hundred dollars, and the insurance company would pay the balance up to the maximum coverage.

Then the insurance company jumped up its rates. I, along with many others, increased my deductible to $500 to get a lower premium. The next year, the company raised its premium by another $450, and if I wanted to keep the same $500 deductible, my premium was $450 more. However, if I were willing to accept a higher $1000 deductible, they would give me the previous year's rate. In other words, I could either pay the premium—or pay the deductible—but either way it was going to cost me around $500.

Except that if I paid the premium, it definitely would cost me the $500. However, if I accepted a higher deductible, in this case $1000, I'd only pay if I had a claim. If I didn't have a claim, I would save almost $500.

I went for the $1000 premium. I know some owners who are accepting $1500 and even $2500 deductibles in order to get that premium down.

What's happening here is that the insurance company is asking the insured to carry part of the risk. If you don't have any claims, it usually works out best for you to take a higher deductible in order to get a lower premium. On the other hand, if you can anticipate more than one claim, paying the higher premium for the lower deductible (which applies separately to each claim) might be more desirable. (See above about cancellations and nonrenewals.)

Playing with Replacement Costs

Normally when you apply for homeowner's insurance, it's based in part on the square footage of your home. Then the insurer makes an estimate of the quality of construction. Typically it's average, medium, or expensive. Finally, using an index for your area and type of construction, it multiplies this to get the estimated replacement cost of your home. This is the amount for which it will insure you.

Often you can't get less unless you sign some sort of waiver. If you want more coverage, it is available, but at a steep premium.

Why would you want more or less than the replacement cost? The reason is that the insurance company's estimates might be way off. For example, I have property in the Sierra mountains of Northern California. When I get insurance, I'm given a replacement cost of around $90 to $100 a square foot. I'm told that because the property is in a rural area in the mountains, it will be cheaper to replace than if it were in an urban area, where similar homes are insured for $150 or more a square foot.

Unfortunately, in the mountains with freezing winters, building requires deep footings for foundations and heavy snow loads for roofs and walls. Construction costs up there are actually far higher than on flat land. I know because I was also recently involved in a building project and our costs ran $160 a square foot!

So where does that leave me IF the property I insured for $100 a square foot burns down? It probably leaves me a bit short. Will the insurance company rebuild my property only up to the roof and stop there because they run out of money?

Actually, when you buy homeowner's insurance these days, you get a variety of different plans. Some are very strict—they only pay off to the maximum insured amount. Others have overage plans—they pay typically up to 125 percent if costs were higher than estimated. And some Cadillac plans (no longer available in many areas) offer guaranteed replacement regardless of what it costs. Be sure to check your policy what it says about replacement—you might want to increase your coverage!

Plans also have different formulas for dealing with inflation and new building codes. Many include an inflation index that automatically raises the maximum coverage to keep in line with inflation. And others guarantee to increase the coverage to meet new building codes. The latter can be a big expense.

For example, let's say your home was built 25 years ago. Back then footings (how deep the foundation has to go into the ground) were only required to go 8 inches deep.

You have a disaster and your house burns down to the ground. You want to rebuild. Only now, the building department tells you that your structure must be rebuilt to current standards, which include 16-inch footings. This one item alone can significantly increase your costs of construction. And there might be many other items. In other words, to replace your old home, it will cost much more (not including inflation) just because of modern building codes. Some policies will cover all, a part, or none of these increases. It would behoove you to know where you stand with your insurer. You might want to switch to a different plan if your insurer offers it. Or you might just want to switch insurers to get a better plan.

Other Concerns

Just because you have insurance, that doesn't mean you're adequately insured. In the haste to buy a home, you might only have obtained the minimum necessary. Or you might have gotten far too much.

Now that you've moved in, you should take the time to find out just what kind of coverage you need, how much you have, and make adjustments. If you have a good insurance agent, he or she can be invaluable in helping you here. If you're on your own, then now's the time to find a good agent.

TIP—USE A PROFESSIONAL

I always suggest that you use a good insurance agent. Yes, you can get insurance cheaper on the Internet. Yes, you can figure out just what you need and buy that directly from insurance companies. However, for what usually is only a little bit more, you are losing out on the experience of someone who knows the field and knows what's available. A good insurance agent can often save you money by tailoring an insurance plan to better serve your needs.

What about Life Insurance?

For homeowners, life insurance can be an excellent tool for handling some estate problems, particularly when there's a matter of paying off death taxes. You should consult a good accountant or tax attorney to see if this is appropriate for you.

Life insurance can also be worthwhile to instantaneously build a large estate for a young person who has children, yet who has not yet had time to amass much wealth. This is particularly the case when you have little equity in your home and a large mortgage.

However, be wary of *life* insurance agents posing as property insurance agents, financial planners, or estate planners. While presuming to analyze your property insurance needs, their every answer might be to buy more life insurance, which you might or might not need. Remember, you want just the right amount of property insurance— no more and no less.

2

When Should You Refinance?

It might seem odd to think about refinancing soon after you buy your new home. However, the timing of a refi is important and it's never too early to consider it. Besides, with the way prices of home have skyrocketed in recent years, you might be able (and want!) to refi right away to get some of your equity out in cash.

When to Refi?

For some owners, this decision is simple—you refi as soon as you can get a lower monthly payment or if you need to take money out. This, however, can sometimes be unwise. It's better to take a few moments and look at consequences. There are usually three variables to consider:

Timing Your Refi

1. Consider refinancing when interest rates drop.
2. Consider refinancing when you need the money now.
3. Consider refinancing when you can qualify, particularly if you're concerned that you might not be able to qualify for a new mortgage in the future.

1. Are Interest Rates Lower?

Perhaps you've heard of the 2 percent rule? A decade ago, before refinancing, owners were always cautioned to observe the "2 percent rule." This rule stated that interest rates had to drop 2 percent before it paid to refinance your home to a new lower rate mortgage. The reason was the high transaction costs of the refinance transaction.

Today, the 2 percent rule is out the window. The reason is that in recent years, no-cost refis have become readily available. Today, the costs for some refinancing have dramatically been reduced. Further, those costs can often be included in the new loan by accepting a slightly higher interest rate.

Thus, today it usually makes sense to refi at any time that you can lower your interest rate and monthly payment without increasing the balance (or dramatically affecting the term) of your mortgage, as long as there are no extra costs.

> **EXAMPLE**
>
> You have a $100,000 mortgage at 7 percent with payments of $665 monthly. You find that you can refinance to a new lower 6 percent mortgage at $600 a month, provided you're willing to pay $2500 in closing costs. However, you ask the lender about no cost mortgages and it says that you can have the same mortgage with no costs or fees to you, provided you are willing to accept a slightly higher 6.375 percent interest rate. The new loan will change your payments to $624 monthly, a savings of $41 over what you were paying, but $24 higher than if you had paid the closing costs. It usually makes sense to go ahead with such a no-cost refi. (Paying the closing costs and getting an even lower payment might make sense if you planned on living in the property a very long time.)

Because of no-cost refis and as interest rates were falling after the turn of the century, many owners were refinancing two, three, sometimes four times a year! I've seen owners do a refi simply to get a monthly savings of $10 a month!

TRAP—PENALTY FOR
REPEAT REFINANCING

To discourage rampant refis, some lenders have begun asking for a penalty for quick turnarounds. This states that if the borrower refis out the new loan within a set period of time (typically six months to three years), there is a penalty of $500 or more. Of course, in a competitive market, many lenders offer refis without this penalty. You just have to shop around.

TIP—REFIS AND
CREDIT RATINGS

There is also some concern that repeat refis could adversely affect your credit. However, this is unlikely as long you don't refi more often than about once every six months.

Of course, as interest rates rise, refinancing makes less sense. There's obviously no monetary advantage in going from a 5.5 percent mortgage to a 6.5 percent one.

2. Do You Need the Money?

A separate reason for refinancing revolves around taking money out of your equity in the property. Most financial advisors suggest that this is a bad idea unless you have a good, specific reason for doing so. (Of course, one person's good reason can be another's frivolity.)

Typical good reasons include using the money to finance an education, home improvement, cover emergency medical or other costs, and in some cases, consolidate long-term debts. The rationale here is that you're putting the money to long-term or emergency usage.

On the other hand, typical bad reasons are to take the money out of the property to purchase a new car, to go on a vacation, or to pay off short-term debt.

The rationale for determining good or bad uses for the money usually revolves around the time factor. A mortgage is a long-term debt, typically 15 to 30 years. On the other hand, buying a car, for example, is typically a short-term purchase. In 5 to 7 years, the car might be worn out and you will need another. Yet if you got money to make the purchase from a refi, you'll be paying on that debt for 15 to 30 years, long after the car is in the junkyard. It normally doesn't make sense to purchase short term and pay for it long term.

Home Improvement—This, on the other hand, is usually considered a good reason to pull money out of your equity. The reason is that you're actually building more equity in the property. Hopefully a home that has been improved will be worth considerably more than an unimproved house. Of course, a lot depends on the nature of the improvement.

TRAP—DON'T OVERIMPROVE

Beware of overimproving your home. You should always consider the neighborhood. Putting more money into your house than your neighbors put into theirs is usually a red-flag warning that you're overimproving.

The timing of home improvements is not usually crucial. However, most people only consider doing this during an up-market. When home prices are climbing, it seems to only make sense to put money into your house. On the other hand, when they are falling, it hardly seems worthwhile (because your house is likely to be worth less tomorrow than it is today).

Keep in mind, however, that most home improvements do not yield a dollar-for-dollar return on money spent. Indeed, with the exception of some kitchen and bath renovations, most home improvements cost far more than they add to the value of your property. (For more details on home improvements, check into *Tips and Traps When Renovating Your Home*, McGraw-Hill, 2000.)

There also could be some tax advantages to taking money out for home improvement. If you used all or part of the refi money to pay for home improvements (and provided you meet certain eligibility requirements such as the home being your principal residence), then points you paid, if you had a transaction charge, might be deductible in the year paid. (Otherwise, they are capitalized over the entire term of the loan.) Other expenses such as title insurance and escrow charges are not normally deductible on your principal residence.

TIP—TAX INFO

Information on taxes provided in this book is strictly for the purpose of giving an overview and should not be relied upon. You should consult with a tax professional for all tax questions regarding your property.

Further, generally speaking, if the money was used to improve the home, then the interest on up to $1 million of the debt is deductible as home mortgage interest. This applies to all the combined mortgages on your home (first, second, etc.).

From a tax perspective, generally speaking if you pull money out of your home other than to build or improve the property, you are limited to $100,000 in debt ($50,000 if single or filing separately) for the interest to be tax deductible. (You also can't have pulled out more than the fair value of your home.)

TIP—IT MIGHT
BE DEDUCTIBLE

Generally speaking, for mortgage interest to be deductible, you must have your name both on the deed to the property and on the mortgage. In other words, you must be the party responsible for paying it back, or risk losing your home if you don't. Further, the home must qualify as your main or second home. (There are specific rules for divided use of your home, home office use, and so forth—see a tax specialist.)

Other Uses—Most people consider spending the money on education to be a good use of money pulled out in a refi. After all, it's a way of investing in the future.

On the other hand, taking a cruise with the funds, though a lot of fun, might end up costing you more in the long run than borrowing and paying back in other ways, such as a noncollateralized loan or credit cards. After all, you'll be paying for that one- or two-week cruise over the next 15 to 30 years, depending on the term of the mortgage. That hardly makes sense.

Is Your Need Immediate?

Sometimes when interest rates fall, there is the urge to refi and pull money out of your home, even if you don't have an immediate need for the money. The idea is that you want to grab onto those great low interest rates. And you can always stick that money in the bank.

Not having an immediate (within six months to a year) use for money pulled out of equity, however, can make little sense. For example, you pull $50,000 in equity out of your home. Now, you might be making payments at 6 percent on this money while it earns 2 percent on the bank. You're actually losing 4 percent of the money to interest payments annually.

On the other hand, many people feel that they would rather have their equity in cash in the bank, instead of in an illiquid property. (Real estate is considered illiquid because you can't always refinance or sell just when you want to.) The problem for most of us, of course, is that while we can always find reasons to spend money in the bank, it's usually more of a hassle to pull money out of equity. Thus, keeping our money in equity might actually be a safer way of saving than keeping it in the bank.

TIP—ACT WHEN RATES ARE DOWN

If you think interest rates are going to climb in the next few years and you have a use for the money in the future, it can make sense to pull out the funds now and lock in the lower rates. It all depends, of course, on IF rates rise and IF you actually go forward with that use.

**TRAP—REFI NOW
AND DON'T PAY
LATER**

If you pull money out of your property now, you might not have the funds available when you later sell to pay any capital gains taxes. (Remember, refinancing does not affect the tax basis of your property.) On the other hand, if it's your personal residence and you live there 2 out of 5 years, you probably can take the up to $500,000 exclusion (per couple filing jointly) on capital gains which can help to mitigate this problem.

Can You Qualify?

Finally, there's the matter of qualifying for a new mortgage. If you recently purchased and since then interest rates have dropped, chances are that you will easily qualify for a new, lower-rate mortgage. After all, you'll be going for lower mortgage payments than you currently have and, assuming your income and credit haven't changed, getting the new mortgage should be a breeze.

On the other hand, if you recently bought and now want to pull money out of your home, it could be trickier. Pulling money out means getting a bigger loan. And a bigger loan often means higher payments. If you just squeaked into your present financing and your financial condition hasn't improved, you might not qualify for a new and bigger loan.

My suggestion is that to find out just where you stand at any given time, you contact a mortgage broker (you probably used one when you bought the property) and get preapproved. If it's been more than three months since your last preapproval, you'll probably need to go through the process again. However, it should be free. (Most mortgage brokers don't charge, except for around $35 for securing a credit report, and many don't charge for that IF you go forward with the loan.) You'll immediately know how big a loan you can get given current interest rates and your present financial condition.

How to Pull Money Out—
The Refinance

The key to being able to refi and pull money out is whether or not your property has gone up in value. For example, if you originally obtained a 100 percent LTV (loan to value) mortgage and prices haven't moved up, there's no way to pull equity out of your property—you don't have any equity!

On the other hand, if since you bought the price of your home has gone up 50 percent, you should have loads of equity you can pull out no matter how big your original mortgage. Usually, before letting you pull equity out, lenders want to see that you have at least 20 percent equity, that the mortgage isn't for more than 80 percent LTV.

EXAMPLE

If your home is valued at $100,000 and you already have an 80-percent LTV loan or $80,000 on it, you probably don't have enough equity in the property to refinance and pull money out. On the other hand, if your home is valued at $125,000, your existing LTV is only about 64 percent and your equity is 36 percent, some of which you can now pull out.

Of course, these figures only apply when you're refinancing to get money out. If you only want to replace the existing mortgage with another (plus any closing costs), financing up to 100 percent of LTV is available.

TIP—CHANGING
RULES

These "rules" are constantly changing. Check with your mortgage broker to see exactly what's available when you apply.

Getting a Second Mortgage

Thus far we've been speaking of refinancing as replacing your existing first mortgage with a new one. However, there's an alternative to this—getting a second mortgage.

In this case, you keep your original loan and add another on top of it called a "second" mortgage. This second might have various names such as a "home equity loan," "home improvement loan," or "revolving line of credit."

TIP—MORTGAGES GO BY ORDINAL NUMBER

You can also get a third mortgage if you already have two. Sometimes you can get even a fourth mortgage. However, because the risk for the lender increases with the higher number of mortgages, usually interest rates also increase. (The risk increases because in any foreclosure the lowest-numbered mortgage is paid off first. If there's any money left over, the next lowest mortgage is paid, and so on. Higher-numbered mortgages risk not getting paid off at all!)

The advantages of getting a second mortgage is that you do not have to disturb the original first mortgage. For example, perhaps interest rates have gone up since you purchased. Your mortgage carries a 5-percent interest rate. But new firsts are at 6 percent.

A new second mortgage might be at 7 percent. Depending on the amount borrowed, it might be cheaper to obtain the higher-interest second, than a new higher interest first.

The way to determine whether it pays to get a new second or a new first is to determine the *blended* interest rate. For example, if you already have a large first mortgage of $100,000 at 5 percent and can get a new smaller second mortgage of $50,000 at 7 percent, the blended rate is roughly 5.5 percent. This is better than getting a new first mortgage of $150,000 at 6 percent.

You have to recalculate each time for the amount of the mortgage and the interest rate. Many online lenders (such as eloan.com) have calculators to help you with this. Also, we're assuming your existing first is only a few years old. If it's an older amortized loan, the pribciple has gone down and there's less interest to be paid.

Disadvantages of a Second Mortgage

There are some disadvantages of getting a second mortgage. Typically the payments will have a shorter term, often 15 years or less. This means that the money payment will be significantly higher than for a longer-term loan at the same interest rate.

Further, the interest rate itself might be so high that it doesn't make sense to go forward with the second. You'll need to check around at different banks and mortgage brokers to find the lowest rate.

Finally, in many cases lenders won't wrap the costs of the refinance into the second, but will want to be paid separately. This certainly can make this loan less attractive.

Variations on a Second Mortgage

Banks will offer a second mortgage or home-equity loan typically in two forms. In the first, you get the money all up-front. In the second you get what is essentially a revolving line-of-credit. You can borrow on your home equity up to certain limits at any time and pay the money back at any time. You are only charged for the time you actually used the money. There is also typically an annual charge for this type of account, although the bank will usually absorb any closing costs.

This is a very versatile type of financing and is excellent when used as a source of emergency money. However, only rarely is the interest rate fixed. Usually the interest rate varies depending on market conditions and tends to be significantly higher than for first mortgages.

Thus, a home equity loan makes good sense to have around for emergency money. But, if you have a specific use, such as home improvement, a different type of loan might be better.

A home-improvement loan might be nothing more than a home-equity loan by a different name. However, some lenders will offer a home improvement loan based on "take as you go." You take out the money as you make your improvements. It's a kind of construction loan. It differs from the home equity loan in that you don't pay it off as you will. You only take money out (although typically you only pay interest on the money withdrawn) and once you've taken it out fully, the loan converts to a longer term (typically 5 to 15 year) lower interest rate loan.

A home improvement loan of the above type can sometimes carry a lower interest rate than a revolving home equity loan. It sometimes can also be insured through HUD (see FHA home improvement loans at www.hud.gov.)

Adjustable versus Fixed-Rate Mortgage

Finally, there's the matter of getting a mortgage with an interest rate that fluctuates according to market conditions, or is fixed for the life of the loan. The advantage of the adjustable rate mortgage is that it carries a lower initial interest rate (sometimes called the "teaser" rate). However, that rate rises as the market for mortgage interest rates rises.

TIP—THE RATE RULE

The general rule is that it pays to lock in low interest rates with a fixed interest rate loan. On the other hand, it pays to get an adjustable rate mortgage when rates are high so that your interest rate will fall as rates generally drift down.

The Federal Reserve Board has complained that too many home loan borrowers rely on the fixed-rate mortgage over the adjustable rate mortgage and that during periods of low interest rates, as we've recently had, this has cost them money. It says that if interest rates do go up, the borrower can always switch.

My own suspicion is that the Fed is more concerned about protecting lenders from spikes in interest rates that it is in saving borrowers a few dollars. If interest rates were to jump up, banks that were carrying low fixed-interest rate loans would stand to be hurt. On the other hand, banks that were carrying adjustable interest rate mortgages would be fine. Their interest rates would climb along with the market. Further, if borrowers were forced to refinance, banks could then cash out their existing lower-rate portfolio of loans.

Unfortunately, the results would be exactly the opposite for homeowner/borrowers. If you have a fixed-rate mortgage, you're happy as a clam when interest rates rise and everyone around you is having trouble. On the other hand, if you have an adjustable rate mortgage and interest rates rise, you're one of those having trouble because your payments will soar.

Having been through periods in this country when mortgage interest rates were above 15 percent, I personally don't worry nearly as much about the banks as I do about borrowers.

TIP—CAPS CAN HELP

Most adjustable interest rates have "caps," which prevent interest rates from rising above a certain maximum amount. (They also have "steps," which limit how fast and big interest rate jumps can be.) However, these caps are typically set very high, often twice or more the original interest rate. If your loan jumps from 5 percent to 10 percent (even if it's done gradually through small steps), your monthly payments are going to skyrocket even with caps. Not a pleasant outcome.

3

Can You Really Improve Your Home's Value through Renovation?

One of the most common scenes today is to see a new home buyer gutting a home even before moving in. It's not just a matter of painting, which most new owners have always done. It's renovating kitchens, bathrooms, entrance halls, even adding space in the form of new bedrooms or living areas. In some cases new home owners will completely insulate, drywall, and then add shelving and cabinets to a garage!

The cost of doing this is phenomenal. Indeed, as noted earlier, according to one representative of Home Depot to whom I spoke, they estimate that the average new home owner will spend $10,000 within the first six months of ownership renovating the property!

Of course, there's nothing wrong with this. You buy a home and you want to remake it into something that suits your own tastes. The new home owner is just creating a nest in which to feel comfortable.

However, underneath usually is the belief that all that renovation is actually adding value. Spending $10,000 or $50,000 or whatever on the home only makes it more valuable and the owner will get all that back, and more, when the home is eventually sold.

The proof of this underlying assumption of added value comes from the fact that home renovation explodes when the real estate market is up, as it has been for the past few years, and comes to a virtual halt when the market is down. During the early-1990s, when real estate prices were falling in many parts of the country, almost no one renovated their homes. Their rationale was, why spend money on a house that could be worth less tomorrow than it's worth today?

Does Renovation Really Add Value?

As a new home owner who's tempted to pour money into home renovation, you should ask yourself an important financial question. Does renovation really add value? Or, even in an up real estate market, am I just pouring money down a rat hole? The answer might surprise you.

In most cases, renovating your home will increase its value. But it will not increase it enough to warrant the renovation. In other words, it will not get you a dollar-for-dollar return. Rather, you might get 20 cents of added value for each dollar you invest. Strictly speaking, in terms of making money, you might be better off "investing" in Las Vegas or Atlantic City gaming casinos.

On the other hand, some very specific kinds of renovations will not only return dollar-for-dollar, but might go over the top, making money for you. However, to find these you have to be very shrewd in evaluating your property.

How Do I Evaluate What to Renovate?

The first step is to make the sometimes difficult separation between what renovation would make you personally feel good, and what renovation (if any) your home really needs. In other words, it's important to divide it into two separate perspectives: personal and financial.

TIP—DON'T GO OVERBOARD

Most people have good instincts in choosing what to renovate. They just tend to go overboard and spend far too much.

When deciding to upgrade, most of us are swayed by what's currently popular in home decorating. Granite countertops, marble flooring, solid wood cabinets, wood-metal double-pane windows—the list is endless. You can upgrade your home easily spending $50,000 to $150,000 or more in just a few rooms!

These quality-renovated homes become showcases where you can entertain friends and enjoy the good life. However, my suggestion is that before pursuing any renovation, large or small, you do a cost versus value analysis. How much will the work actually add to the value of the property? Does what you are going to do make financial sense?

TRAP—DON'T CREATE A WHITE ELEPHANT

A "white elephant" in the real estate trade is a home that has been overbuilt for its neighborhood. The owners have put far more in than they can realistically hope to get out.

The Appreciation Argument Trap

Before considering what's worthwhile to do and what's not, let's spend a moment considering home appreciation. I was just talking with a neighbor who's spending $200,000 on the finest in home upgrades. She comes right out and says that she knows she's overdoing it for the neighborhood. But, then she says, "I just hope that prices will go up until I can get my money out."

This is an argument that most people use to justify overrenovating their home. Prices of properties are going up, so they will eventually be able to get their money out. It's important to understand that this argument makes little sense.

If prices of real estate in your area are going up, then they are doing so whether or not you renovate. The renovation doesn't make the prices go up; the marketplace competition for homes does. Yes, a renovated house will tend to sell quicker and for more money, but it will do so at every price range. What drives prices higher are fewer homes and more buyers, supply and demand.

For example, your home is worth $500,000 and you put $100,000 in renovation into it. Now, is it worth $600,000? Perhaps it is. But what if your neighbor next door who has the exact same house, but did no renovation at all, can sell for $580,000? How much did your renovation add to the value of your home and how much did market appreciation? (The answer is the market forced it up $80,000 and your $100,000 of work added an additional $20,000 to the home's value —just a 20-percent return.)

TRAP—DON'T CONFUSE MARKET APPRECIATION WITH INVESTMENT RETURN

It's a mistake to believe that prices going up financially justifies doing expensive work on your house. Prices might go up even if you didn't do the work.

If you honestly do care about the value added to your home by a renovation project, you should do a careful evaluation *before you start* to see just what the figures are. That way you can accurately put a price on the two factors: financial and personal.

TIP—MAKING MONEY COUNTS

No matter how much a home owner protests that he or she doesn't care about values and is only doing renovation work to satisfy themselves, I've never met anyone who liked to lose money on their home. Yes, renovate to make your home more comfortable and livable. But keep in mind that a home is also an investment, one on which you'd like to make a profit.

How Do I Determine What Renovations Are Justified for My Home?

Before getting the first bid from a contractor, I suggest you consider four separate areas:

Areas to Consider

- Neighborhood
- Price range of the house
- Age
- Market condition

Neighborhood, Neighborhood, Neighborhood

If the three most important considerations when buying a house are location, location, location, than neighborhood represents the three most important when renovating. The point here is that you want to be able to sell your home at some time. And how much you'll be able to sell it for is determined mostly by your neighborhood.

TRAP—IT'S ONLY FOR A SHORT TIME

Many people buy their home with the idea that they're going to live there forever. Statistically, however, most people sell their homes within 7 to 9 years, depending on the area of the country in which they live. If you can think of your home as only a temporary residence, at least for financial purposes, you'll go a long way toward making the right renovation decision.

As you probably learned when making offers to buy homes, price is determined by doing a comparison of recent sales. You see what comparable homes have sold for in the area, and then you extrapolate what the house in question is worth. You deduct a bit if the house is run-down, add a bit if it's renovated, and that gives you (and ultimately the buyer of your home), the price.

Thus, the first thing you should do before renovating is tour your neighborhood. Get to know your neighbors and where possible, get to see their homes. Find out what they've done in terms of renovation.

For example, if everyone has added a bonus room (perhaps because the homes are simply too small), then this will automatically be calculated into market pricing. Your home *without* a bonus room will take longer to sell for possibly much less money. Your home *with* a bonus room will sell quicker and, presumably, for at least as much as its neighbors. The same holds true right down the line with every change made to the home that differs from the original floor plan and design.

Of course, this rule works best with tract homes where there are many similar properties. It's far less reliable in areas of custom homes where every house is different. Nevertheless, it can be applied in custom homes as well. For example, if all the custom homes in an area have a built-in pool or spa, you probably can justify putting one in yourself. If your home doesn't have it, it will probably not sell for as much (if nothing else, on a square-foot basis) than its neighbors. With it, it will be able to compete in the marketplace.

The whole idea of visiting your neighbors' homes is not to admire their improvements; it's to get a feeling for what the home renovation standards for your neighborhood are. In some areas, there will be few to no improvements. In others every home will be renovated. Take your cue from your neighborhood. It will tell you what you should—and shouldn't—do.

Price Range of the Home

The simple truth of the matter is that the higher the price range of your home, the more renovation you can usually justify. If yours is an average-priced home of $180,000, then it hardly makes sense to spend $50,000 on a kitchen renovation. On the other hand, if yours is a $700,000 home, then putting $50,000 into the kitchen might make perfectly good sense.

The amount of money you can justify sinking into a home should be determined, at least in part, by the price of the home. This does not mean, of course, that there's no point in renovating less expensive homes. It only means that the cost of the renovation should correspondingly be less expensive.

Of course, prices vary enormously by areas of the country. In some parts of the coasts, $300,000 won't buy you anything but a shack. In parts of the Midwest and the South, on the other hand, it can buy you a palace.

Regardless of the area, however, there are always homes that are at the low end, in the middle, and at the high end. And regardless of the pricing relative to your area, the general rule is that you can afford to renovate more in a high-end home than in a low-end one.

Age of the Home

If your home is relatively new, the chances are that it will need little renovating, with the possible exception of something that was left out or done awkwardly. On the other hand, if your home is 10 or more years old, then the chances are that some renovation is in order. Homes 30 and more years old might need major restoration, sometimes involving tearing out previous renovations and modernizing them.

The effect of the renovation likewise is related to the age. The amount of bounce you'll get in price by renovating an older home should be much more than what you'll get from doing a newer property. If the home is very old, say 80 years or more, and in a good area, you'll probably get far more than dollar-for-dollar return on many renovations. Indeed, in very old homes, the price is often significantly discounted if the home has not been updated.

The Market Condition

Finally, there's the matter of market timing. We touched on this earlier. When the market's hot and prices are rising, you're more likely to get money out of your renovation than if the housing market is cold and prices are falling.

This only makes sense. In a depressed market buyers simply won't want to spend extra bucks for the extra work you did. In a hot market, they will. All of which is to say that it makes more sense to renovate in hot, rather than cold, markets.

Four Rules of Renovating

---

1. Don't overbuild for the neighborhood.
2. Don't spend more than the price range warrants.
3. Older houses return more on renovation than newer ones.
4. It's better to renovate in a hot market than a cold one.

What Type of Renovation Should I Do?

Always renovate what needs remodeling. This might sound simple-minded, but it carries a lot of wisdom. If your kitchen is old-fashioned, renovate it. Don't look at the kitchen, discover that the costs are going to be expensive, and so instead renovate the bathroom, which might or might not need it.

Bite the bullet. If all the other kitchens in your neighborhood have been redone, redo yours. You don't have to make it the most elaborate renovation. But simply ignoring it turns it into a downgrading feature of your home.

**TRAP—DON'T
CONFUSE REPAIR
WITH RENOVATION**

If you have a broken window, replacing it is not renovating. It's repairing. Similarly, if the furnace doesn't work, you've got broken tiles, the door on the oven is broken, fix it all. But don't think you're renovating (unless you replace with a more modern or better item). Some things simply must be done to maintain the home in its current condition. Renovating means improving that condition.

Spend a lot of time looking. Go to building supply stores like Lowes and Home Depot. They typically have showrooms displaying a variety of different renovating options for many different rooms in the house. Check out specialty stores that sell appliances and fixtures. They, too, often have displays that showcase how items will look in the home and how various different pieces will look together. (See the Appendix.)

Call in an interior designer to give you ideas. Even if you don't later use the designer, the ideas you get might be eye openers. A professional can often spot areas that are in desperate need of renovation that you might otherwise simply overlook. (It's sort of like getting a professional stylist to do a face or hair makeover—the results can be far different, and hopefully far better, than you might have imagined on your own.)

Check out magazines on home redecorating and renovation. The shelves at newsstands and in bookstores are clogged with them. Look at the pictures. See what others have done. No, you don't need to copy anyone else's design. But, the new ideas you see there might lead you to creative options for your home that you might not otherwise have considered.

Call in *many* contractors who specialize in home renovation, not just to give you bids, but to give you ideas. An experienced professional can sometimes simply walk through your house and say, "you need a skylight there," or, "a counter should go there." Their quick insights can turn you around 180 degrees in your thinking. Of course, later you might want to use these same contractors to do the work, or not. Most such estimates and bids are given free, or at nominal costs.

TIP—A SET OF PLANS
WILL HELP

Don't be afraid to spend money on plans and ideas before you actually start your project. Once you actually begin work, it's usually too late (or too costly) to be creative.

Also, don't overlook the advice a real estate agent can offer. This professional sees homes on a constant basis and might have a better idea than anyone else of what sells and what doesn't. A good agent walking through a home and being candid with you can sometimes make simple suggestions that will add thousands to the value, of your home, yet only cost hundreds to accomplish.

Should I Do Some or All of the Work Myself?

If you can afford it, my advice is to hire it all out. There are good reasons why:

Reasons to Hire It Out

- You'll get a professional looking job.
- You won't injure yourself.
- It should be done properly and up to building code.
- You can concentrate on the design, not the work.

On the other hand, if you're handy, you might want to do some or all of a project on your own. If you do it yourself, however, remember to *pay yourself* a reasonable salary, else you'll mistakenly think you're getting it done far cheaper than the actual costs.

Also, be sure that you know what you're doing. Apparently, simple jobs like taping and texturing drywall require special skills. And others such as installing electrical fixtures or plumbing in sinks need to be done correctly to avoid health and safety problems. *Be sure the power is completely off before doing any electrical work.* It will do you no good to apparently save money by doing it yourself if the result is shoddy looking or unsafe work that any eventual home buyer will want replaced.

TIP—GET A PERMIT

No matter who does the work, be sure it's done with the benefit of a building permit. This requires plans, paying a fee, getting a permit, and having the work inspected. However, later on when you go to sell and the buyer demands that you produce a building permit, or rip out the work and cut your price, you won't have a problem. (It should also help in liability issues as well.)

TRAP—DON'T
TAKE RISKS

If you do any work yourself, be sure to observe common safety rules. For example, never work on electrical fixtures or appliances unless the power is off. Never do work on plumbing or gas unless it is properly tested for safety before being turned on. Be aware that some jurisdictions prohibit homeowners from doing their own work on electrical, gas, plumbing, and other areas of home improvement.

Finally, many people, your author included, like to do renovation work themselves simply for the love of it. If you're in that group, then I encourage you to try it. Chances are you'll do well and be very pleased with the outcome. And if not, you can always hire somebody to fix it!

Which Areas Will
Add the Most Value?

This, of course, is the big question that most people ask. Which improvements are money pits and which yield a good return on investment?

If you want an honest answer, in most cases, all renovations are money pits of one sort or another. Very few, if any, will yield at least a dollar-for-dollar return.

The exception is when a home has a defect. For example, you have a very dark living room or family room. It's just the way the house was designed.

Putting a new window in a wall or adding a skylight to add more light to the room might often add far more to the value of the home than the cost of the renovation. The reason is that it will make the overall house more salable and more desirable to buyers, who will be willing to pay more for it.

If your home has an identifiable defect, such as the dark room noted above or a single bathroom (when almost all buyers want a minimum of two bathrooms), don't hesitate to correct it. Unless you don't go overboard, you should be adding more than it costs to your home's value.

Kitchens—The Most Valuable Area

The closest you likely can come to a dollar-for-dollar return on your investment is by renovating a kitchen. This, of course, is provided that you don't go overboard and spend more than your neighborhood or home's price range warrants (see earlier comments).

Kitchen renovations tend to the most expensive. On the other hand, as noted, they also tend to give you more buck for your bang. The reason is that in today's modern family, the kitchen has become the center of the home. Even if the family doesn't do much actual cooking, the kitchen has become the meeting place, the spot where homework is often done, where chats are conducted over coffee, and the showplace when you bring neighbors and friends in to see your home. Thus, sparkling kitchens in new and expensive woods and stone with high-tech appliances help sell a house for more money.

A complete kitchen renovation means tearing everything out to the bare walls and starting off from scratch. It can include:

Kitchen Renovation

- New countertops (granite, Corian®, tile, Formica®)
- New cabinets (real and composite woods)
- New fixtures (plain to exotic designs and functions)
- New appliances (electric, gas, high-tech)
- New lighting (recessed, florescent, natural)
- New flooring (real or composite woods, stone, tile)

As soon as you begin pricing all of the above, you'll quickly see why a kitchen is easily the most expensive place to renovate a home. (The only exception being when you create additional space by building an addition.)

If you go all the way and get granite countertops, hardwood cabinets, top-of-the line fixtures and appliances, natural (by means of skylights) and recessed lighting, and natural wood or stone flooring, you've just spent the better part of $50,000 to $60,000 on a kitchen. Spending well over $100,000 is not difficult.

If your home is valued at $750,000 or more and if it's in a highly desired neighborhood of mostly renovated homes, you'll probably get most of your money back. On the other hand, if your home is more modestly priced, then a more modest renovation might be in order.

For example, here's a renovation for a $200,000 home that cost a total of around $10,000 and probably came close to adding dollar-for-dollar to the value of the property.

Modest Kitchen Renovation	
▪ Tile countertops	$2,500
▪ Pressed wood cabinets	$4,500
▪ Standard sink and fixtures	$600
▪ Standard appliances	$1,500
▪ Florescent lighting	$500
▪ Linoleum flooring	$500
	$10,100

This modest renovation was perfectly suited to the price range of the home in which it was made and added roughly dollar-for-dollar to its value. Compare this with a more elegant kitchen renovation:

Elegant Kitchen Renovation	
▪ Granite countertops	$17,500
▪ Hardwood cabinets	$19,000
▪ Elegant sink and fixtures	$4,500
▪ Top-of-the line appliances	$6,000
▪ Recessed lighting	$9,800
▪ Natural wood flooring	$6,700
	$63,500

The elegant renovation was done to a home in the $700,000 price range. It actually helped boost the value closer to a million dollars. (Some said the renovation wasn't elegant enough!)

The point here is that you probably can get back most of the money you "invest" in a kitchen, provided you suit the renovation to the price of the home (and, of course, the neighborhood). Don't overbuild. Don't get carried away with what you'd personally love to have in your home. Instead, renovate with an eye toward reselling.

TIP—BETTER TO SELL THAN TO OVERBUILD

What's wrong with spending whatever you want to renovate with what you'd personally want in a house? Nothing, unless you like to lose money. If what you'd like overbuilds for the home and the neighborhood, my suggestion is that you sell and buy a better house in a better area more realistically suited to your tastes.

Bathrooms—The Second Most Valuable Area

Most people today love bathrooms. Just check out the models at any new home tract. You'll see spacious baths, especially off the master bedroom. Indeed, the bathrooms of today often are bigger than the bedrooms of yesterday!

After a kitchen, the next best place to spend money on a renovation usually is the bathroom. If your home comes with a dingy little bathroom and you're able to expand its size (as well as put in new fixtures), you might actually get more than dollar-for-dollar on your costs. Of course, it depends on how you're able to expand it. Adding onto your house is very expensive and seldom, if ever, can you get all your costs back. On the other hand, if you're clever and expand the bathrooms by cannibalizing a part of another bedroom or closet or other storage space, it's a different story. Assuming no severe structural changes are necessary, expanding into other areas can be relatively inexpensive and can sometimes yield fabulous results.

Here's what you'll want to consider doing to a master bathroom:

Master Bathroom Do Over
■ Expand the size.
■ Put in double sinks.
■ Put the toilet in a separate enclosed area.
■ Have separate tub and shower.
■ Add new lighting.
■ Install new cabinets and tops.
■ Use all new plumbing fixtures.
■ As an added bonus, you might also want to expand the closet space in the master bedroom.

The cost of expanding and fixing up a modern bathroom can easily be as much as renovating a kitchen. Usually prices, however, are a bit more moderate. Before rushing out to spend $30,000 on your bathroom, however, be sure to reconsider the guidelines we've suggested. Take into consideration the value of your house, its age, the real estate market, and of course what's normally been done in your neighborhood.

TIP—REMEMBER THE 5-PERCENT BATHROOM RULE

It's hard to justify spending more than about 5 percent of your home's value on the bathroom. For a $500,000 house that's $25,000. On a $200,000 house, however, that's only $10,000. The less you spend, but the better it looks, the more you will have increased your equity in your home.

Other Areas to Renovate

The list, of course, is endless. Here's a list of some of the more popular areas to renovate, along with their potential for adding value to your home, and their payback:

Project Possible Max Payback*	
▪ Attic conversion	75%
▪ Basement completion	75%
▪ Bathroom renovation (master)	65%
▪ Bedroom addition	50%
▪ Deck addition	35%
▪ Den addition	50%
▪ Family room addition	50%
▪ Front door—adding new	110%
▪ Home office conversion	75%
▪ Interior doors—upgrading	50%
▪ Kitchen renovation	95%
▪ Patio addition	50%
▪ Pool (new)	45%
▪ Spa (new)	55%

* The actual value added will depend on a large number of factors, including the age of the home, its price range, its condition, the market, and what's normally done in the neighborhood.

**TRAP—DO IT NOW,
DO IT LATER
A SECOND TIME**

Always keep in mind the time frame. If you do a renovation today and live in the home for another 10 years, it might very well be ready for a second renovation by the time you decide to sell.

The Driving Force

Renovating a home soon after moving in is sort of a nesting complex. It's the way we make the house into our own. And because it's going to be our special place, we are often driven to spend unwarranted amounts of money on our various renovation projects.

Try to remember that this house is only temporary. Eventually, you will move and it will become someone else's home. And the sooner you're likely to move, the less you'll want to spend making it over into a place only for you.

That's, of course, the financial perspective. But, as I said before, I've never met anyone who liked to lose money on his or her property. Overspending on home renovation can be throwing funds, often needed elsewhere, into the wind.

TIP—LOOK TO COSMETIC CHANGES

 The quickest way to add value to your home through renovation is to make cosmetic changes. Paint, detergent, and flowers almost always add far more than their cost to the home.

4

Watching Out for Value Grabbers

Once escrow closes and you move into your beautiful new home (even if it's only new to you!), you can relax with regard to property values, right? Hopefully, if the market stays good, the only thing you need check is the annual price appreciation.

Wrong!

While most of us still believe that a person's home is his or her castle, realistically today's castle has lots of holes in its walls. There are all sorts of external influences that can positively or adversely affect your property's value. These include:

Neighborhood Influences on Home Values

- Planning department and zoning changes
- Homeowner's Association's rules and regulations
- Nuisances in the area

In order to preserve and protect your home's value, you might need to take a more active role than you anticipated or wanted. You might have to talk to and organize neighbors, sign petitions, attend meetings, and more.

But, you might be thinking to yourself, that's not what I signed up for! Maybe not, but then again, that's why you're reading this book, to find out all the things they didn't tell you when you became a new home buyer.

Planning Department Changes

I'm sure that many new home owners are wondering how and why the planning department of their city or county could have an influence on their existing home's value. Aren't the zoning laws that regulate land use set in stone? Why should anyone worry about this?

Actually, zoning laws, which for example determine if a lot can have a single-family residence or an industrial plant built on it, are much more nebulous than most people realize. While today most communities do have a master plan that the city officials (read planning commission, city council, board of supervisors, and so on) are supposed to follow, sometimes there can be variances.

TIP—SOME VARIANCES DO PASS

While zoning laws are designed to protect property owners from poor use of nearby land, there's nothing to keep a would-be developer from asking for a "variance." This is a single-case change to the zoning laws. To take an extreme example, a developer might ask for the right to put a toxic waste dump in the lot next to your home. No, it's not likely to pass the planning commission, which usually oversees zoning laws. But "not likely" isn't "never" or "guaranteed no." Some variances, such as allowing development of strip malls at the edge of residential areas, do pass with surprising frequency, even though they might have an adverse impact on neighboring properties.

Zoning Laws and CC&Rs

Almost certainly your home is covered by two sets of rules. The first, zoning laws, we've already begun discussing. The second, called CC&Rs (Conditions, Covenants, and Restrictions) are imposed by the developer of your property and run with the title. That means that they are rules that go with your home and that you cannot change (at least not easily), but instead must live by. CC&Rs often specify the color you may paint your home, the number of stories it can have, the minimum square footage, and so on. They are used to help maintain neighborhood standards.

TRAP— DISCRIMINATION IN CC&Rs IS ILLEGAL

 Years ago, some developers used to regularly include discrimination clauses in CC&Rs such as restricting the right to ownership of the home of certain ethnic, racial, or religious groups. These discrimination clauses have long been ruled invalid, yet they sometimes continue to exist in the CC&Rs. If you come across them, just think of them as a reminder of a distant, different, and less pleasant world. They should have no effect today, but removing them can be such a bureaucratic nightmare that it's sometimes easier to just let them remain in the CC&Rs.

In the absence of an active homeowner's association, it often falls to the planning department to administer not only the zoning laws of the community, but the CC&Rs of your housing development. But, you might reasonably be asking, what does this have to do with me as a new home owner? Let's take an example from real life.

In my own neighborhood, all of the houses are single story. Not having to climb stairs up or down is an advantage to some homeowners, particularly more mature ones or those with physical disabilities. Therefore, this tends to be a highly desired area among a certain group of home buyers, and this has caused prices to appreciate nicely.

However, because they are only a single story, the homes tend to be smaller. And some owners, particularly those with families, would like to add a second story to make their homes larger.

Adding a second story means that the homeowner who did this could take advantage of the existing desirability of our neighborhood, plus command a much higher price because he or she would offer a much larger home.

What's the harm in this?

The answer is that it would change the character of the neighborhood. As soon as one homeowner successfully built a second story, dozens of others would follow suit. Instead of a highly desirable community of single-story homes, we'd have a community of mixed housing types, similar to most other communities. Our uniqueness would be lost—and so would our price advantage.

However, our CC&Rs specifically state that only one-story buildings may be erected. The character of our neighborhood is thus protected.

Nevertheless, one new home owner appealed for a variance. She went before the planning commission, said she needed a bigger home to accommodate her family, and wanted to add a second floor of equal size to her current home, thus doubling its square footage.

Trying to be accommodating, chances are the planning commission would have agreed, had not a host of her neighbors descended on the meeting to protest. They explained that this was a community largely of retired people who bought in the anticipation that all the homes would retain their single-story character. They pointed out that adding a second story would affect the sight-lines and views of her neighbors. They indicated that it could ultimately result in lowering property value. And, that if this new home owner wanted a larger two-story home, she should have bought one.

This is not to say that the homeowner who wanted a variance didn't have some clout on her side. She had a valid reason for expanding her home, her larger family. And in today's tight market (fewer homes than buyers in some areas), adding on made economic sense.

Nevertheless, in this case the CC&Rs specifically excluded anything but single-family homes. And to grant a variance, the planning commission (ever politically sensitive) would have to rule against more than a dozen angry, protesting homeowners, in favor of one homeowner who, ultimately, wanted to boost the value of her property. Guess who won?

The moral behind this story is not that as a new home owner you might find it difficult to put on a second story (although you probably will). It's that you must be very vigilant, watching for changes that could adversely affect your neighborhood and, indirectly, your home's value.

How Do You Know When There's a Change Coming?

There are many ways. If a zoning or CC&R variance is being applied for and your property is directly adjacent to the affected property, you "should" get a notice and an opportunity to attend a planning department meeting where you can voice your opinion.

I say "should" because too often these notices somehow fail to get sent, which leads to your second method of being warned. I call it the neighborhood alarm.

TRAP—IT'S CALLED "SEWER SERVICE"

Instead of serving you the notice, the server somehow manages to drop it down the sewer. So you aren't directly informed.

Chances are there are one or two people in the neighborhood who are nosy. I say this in a kind rather than a pejorative way. They always keep track of what's going on with other people's business. And they often are the first to learn of changes coming involving zoning or CC&Rs, and spread the alarm.

While the tendency is to dismiss these neighborhood sentinels as simply busy bodies, that would be a mistake. If they come by to let you know that something's afoot and ask you to attend a city council meeting, listen to what they say. Evaluate it. Make some calls. And attend the meeting. It's not just your civic duty, it might be a way to protect your property's value.

A third method of finding out about changes in the works is to subscribe to and religiously read your local newspaper. Almost all communities have a local paper, even if it's only a weekly. And typically these papers are starving for news that affects the community. Any zoning change often gets a story. And if you are alert and catch that story, you can let your neighbors know and, if the change is going to adversely affect you, sound out while there's still time to do something about it.

Do I Need to Take Action?

I'm sure that as a new home owner, you envisioned yourself as relaxing in your chair or hammock and enjoying the good life in your new home. Certainly that's part of homeownership. But being ever vigilant is also part of it. To that end, I suggest the following:

How to Keep Vigilant and Protect Your Home's Value

- As mentioned, listen to the neighborhood busy bee and read the local newspaper.
- Read all mail that comes from your city, county, or other government agencies—read all flyers and postings.
- Become friendly with your neighbors. If there's a neighborhood association, join it. Make the time to find out what's going on.
- When there's a meeting affecting CC&Rs or zoning, make a point to attend. Speak out if something will adversely affect you.

As I said, it's not just your civic duty to do all this. It's in your own self-interest.

Should I Join My Homeowner's Association?

If you bought a condo, you have a homeowner's association that you automatically belong to. However, many single-family owners also belong to a HOA. And, if you bought into a co-op, there's a board of directors, similar to an HOA, that watches over your development.

You should know if there's an HOA involved in your neighborhood and home. As part of the documents you received at closing (or before), you should have gotten a packet from your HOA that contained, among other things, a copy of the CC&Rs, the HOA rules and regulations, and probably a letter of welcome. Furthermore, you'll be paying a certain fee each month to the HOA.

You choices with regard to the HOA are usually the following:

- Ignore it and hope that it's benign.
- Attend meetings and speak your piece.
- Join the board and help direct things.

If you're part of an HOA, I suggest you avoid the first, and do the second two, if for no other reason than as a matter of self-protection. HOAs that are poorly led can sometimes cause untold harm to neighborhoods and developments. On the other hand, with good direction, an HOA can help improve property values. Let's take an example:

In one HOA in which I am member, when I bought the property the board was lax and inactive. There was only one general meeting a year, the annual one, in which financial considerations where discussed (mainly how much to pay for insurance and where to hold the annual picnic). Bimonthly meetings mainly were held to rubber-stamp the work of the property manager who supervised the operation of the association.

However, the association faced many challenges: There was a lawsuit from a former employee and a lawsuit from a member who felt that a commonly held walkway was encroaching on his property. There were also demands from a nearby property owner who wanted to allow tenants of a proposed huge apartment building to have access through our streets.

The property manager's method of dealing with all this was to delay and ignore. He delayed dealing with the lawsuits until it became clear that the plaintiffs (the HOA was the defendant) would win, and he ignored requests for a meeting with the developer until it became clear that the apartment building's tenants would drive through our streets by default.

The results of doing nothing could have been calamitous to the value of the homes in the association. Increased traffic on the streets would certainly have reduced the desirability of the neighborhood. And losing lawsuits would mean having to pay damages that would result in higher fees for the homeowners, which again would have made the properties less desirable to buyers (who would have looked askance at both the fees and the lost lawsuits).

Therefore, it meant grabbing the bull by the horns. I and other interested homeowners became involved. We got a new manager, a new attorney, and eventually defeated the lawsuits. We negotiated with the developer and a new road around our development was built. And our property values continued to rise.

The moral here is that an HOA can act for the betterment or the detraction of the members. And, as is the case with a planning department, as a new home buyer, you might need to wade in and help get things going in the right direction.

What You Should Do

This does not mean that your HOA is off track and leading your members on the road to disaster. Most HOAs, indeed, tend to be fairly well run. It's just that you should take time from your busy schedule to be sure.

Find out when the meetings are held and attend a couple. You'll quickly find out whether things are running well or not. (I've been to some HOA meetings where things got so out of hand that there were actual fisticuffs between members!)

Call a few of the board members and speak to them. Ask about current and past issues. Ask about complaints and lawsuits. Ask about the manager's success at handling problems. You'll probably be pleasantly surprised at how willing the board member will be to inform you.

Finally, if things seem out of control or are spiraling downward, don't hesitate to jump in and help control the situation. The property you save might be your own.

Neighborhood Nuisances

Finally, there's the matter of neighborhood nuisances. You just bought your home and it's lovely. The houses on either side of you are well kept. But one house up the street has weeds for a lawn and dead plants for shrubs. It needs paint and soon. Worse, there's another in almost as bad condition on the next block, and another like it a few blocks over.

You get the idea. While your neighborhood might seem generally nice and serene (else why would you want to live there?), parts of it are not so nice. Some homes are actual nuisances in their appearance.

So why should you worry about your neighbor's house? The reason is that those old three words you've heard over and over with regard to real estate: "location, location, location."

When it comes time to sell your present home, potential buyers will evaluate your property, but even more, they'll evaluate your neighborhood. And if your neighborhood is found lacking, no matter how desirable your home might be, it won't command top dollar. In short, neighborhood nuisances will drag down the value of your home.

But, why worry about that now, just after you've moved in? The reason is that it can take a long time to get rid of the nuisances. Sometimes it can take years. And the time to start is sooner rather than later.

If you have a homeowner's association already in place, then that's where to begin. However, chances are if you bought a single-family home, you don't have an HOA. That means you and neighbors you can enlist will have to do the heavy lifting. Getting rid of a neighborhood nuisance can involve all of the following:

Getting Rid of a Neighborhood Nuisance

- **Speak to the offending homeowner.** Maybe the property is a rental and the owner isn't aware that the tenant's let it run down. Or maybe the owner has some financial or health issues that are causing the situation. You might be able to suggest public or private agencies that can provide relief.

- **Speak to your neighbors.** You don't live in a vacuum. If you see the problems, others do too. Perhaps there's already an association of neighbors working to remove it. Join. If not, perhaps you need to start one.

- **Speak to the city.** Sometimes building and safety as well as the planning department can speak to offending owners and pressure them to clean up their act.

- **Consider taking legal action.** When a property is so run-down that it's a nuisance, often the owner is disregarding CC&Rs. You and your neighbors might need to organize to take legal action against the offending owner to convince him or her to set things straight.

Once again, it might seem that I'm asking you to do far more than you signed up for when you bought your home. However, I'm only pointing out what every homeowner faces. The only difference here is that you might be new to the game.

The Neighborhood Challenge

When we buy a home, we all face a challenge. That challenge is to see our neighborhood improve, or deteriorate. (Over time, few neighborhoods remain exactly the same.) You can always choose to do nothing. However, your choice might be reflected in a lower value for your property when it's time to resell.

Taking an active roll, on the other hand, does have demands, mainly on your time. As we've seen, it can mean being gregarious, getting out there and meeting and even organizing your neighbors. It can mean spending a night or two a month attending relevant meetings. It can mean nosing around to find out what's happening in your area, who is trying to sneak what by the planning commission or the HOA. And it can sometimes mean going head-to-head with another homeowner, developer, or other interested party to defend your own interests.

I hope nobody told you that owning a home was going to be a piece of cake, because often it's not. There are plenty of things that you'll want to do to make sure your neighborhood is a great place to live. Of course, others will see the same thing, and that should mean a much better value for your property when it's eventually time to sell.

5

Record Keeping and Tax Deductions for Homeowners

The big problem with record keeping for me is deciding what to keep and what to throw out. In the past I've typically thrown out receipts that, years later, I've discovered I should have saved. And, contrarily, I've saved items for decades that I never have, and never will, use. How does one decide what to save and what to keep?

The answer that I've discovered over the years is linked to the reason for saving it. If you can identify why something should be saved, you can categorize it and then hold it an appropriate amount of time. This also gives you a clear conscience when throwing out something you're unlikely to need. I've come up with several categories that I've found helpful as a homeowner.

Categories for Record Keeping

- Tax-deductible items–Keep receipts long term.

- Receipts for returns and for my credit purchases–Keep receipts at least a year.

- Utility expenses–Keep receipts at least 90 days (unless tax deductible).

What Form Should My Records Take?

Before looking into the specific items that you might want to keep under each category, let's take time to consider the act of keeping records itself. There are two basic methods of record keeping. The first is to create a list of items that you've bought or paid for which you will want to be able to access. For example, when it's time to do your taxes in April, it's very handy to have a list of deductible items that you can quickly look at without having to spend half a day searching through shoe boxes for receipts.

The tried and true method here is the register, a book into which you register each item in pen. The trouble with this is that unless you were very careful to create lots of distinct categories, and unless you've got good handwriting, you're likely to fall into the trap of not knowing why you bought it and not being able to read the entry anyway. Besides, who has time to sit down and make written entries in a book these days?

A more modern (and to my mind vastly better method) is to use a computer program. The majority of homes now have computers, and some very common programs that can be useful will run on most computers. Two that I've found particularly easy to use and helpful are Quicken and Microsoft's MS Money. Both allow you to set up electronic accounts for each of your home record keeping categories. (See Figure 5.1.)

Perhaps the easiest way to handle these is to use one main account for all your bills paid by check and another paid by credit card. Let's consider checks.

In both of these programs you designate a category for each check, such as "House Taxables." At the end of the year (or whenever you're curious), you can simply call up all of the checks written for any particular category and you have an extremely accurate accounting of what you paid to whom (and if you've used notation on the checks, why). This has the added advantage of a single entry because the record is created at the same time as you write your checks.

Of course, most of us pay for many things by charge, rather than cash. These entries will not appear on our electronic record

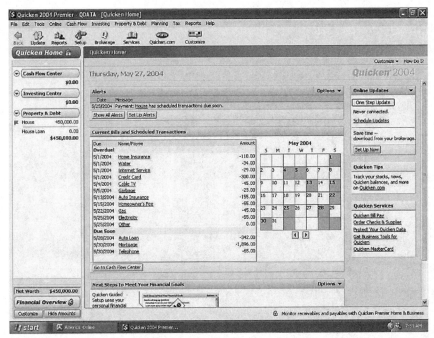

FIGURE 5.1   Quicken Premier 2004 showing categories easily established for home accounts.

keeping program unless we enter them. Thus, you simply create a separate "Charge Card Account" and do the same to it as you would for checks.

TIP—KEEP SEPARATE ACCOUNTS FOR EACH CHARGE CARD

There's no reason that each card you have can't have it's own account. Or, if you want to be clever, you can categorize one charge account in terms of both the card used AND the category of household expense. These programs can easily be manipulated to fit your specific needs.

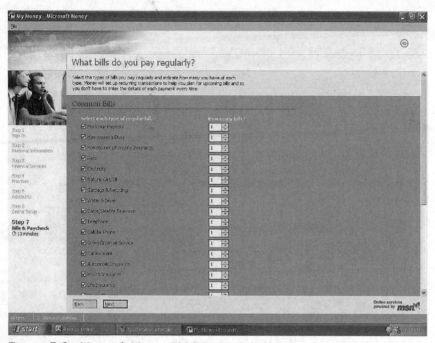

Figure 5.2 Microsoft Money 2004 Premium lets you quickly set up home accounts.

Thus, you can quickly and easily have a record of everything you bought and paid for. However, there is one problem, here. (See Figure 5.2.)

How Do I Document My Records?

It's one thing to have an accurate electronic record of every purchase and bill paid. It's another to actually prove, for example to the IRS, that you actually spent the money. For that you often need a paper trail.

A paper trail consists of checks cashed by the other party and canceled through your bank. It also might require receipts from a vendor. And you might need statements from your credit card company showing charges and payments.

TRAP—SHOULD YOU RELY ON YOUR BANK TO KEEP YOUR RECORDS?

I've always suggested that you keep your canceled paper check as a record of your transaction. That way if the IRS, a merchant, a contractor, or anyone to whom you've paid wants proof of that payment, you have it in hard copy. However, in October of 2004 new legislation was scheduled to go into effect called "Check 21," which alows banks to make an electronic image of your check and then destroy it, in effect turning it into an electronic transfer. In short, banks no longer are required to return your checks. However, banks have long maintained that their electronic records are inviolate and that if you ever need proof of a transfer, they will send you a copy. I tried that once, and the bank sadly informed me that the electronic record had somehow been lost—tough luck. The new law does allow you to request "substitute checks" (photocopies) from your bank, for a fee, which are supposed to be "legible" and have the legal standing of the originals. My suggestion is that you consider getting these substitute checks in order to create a "paper trail," even though the new law also provides additional protections for electronic transfers.

To keep a paper trail I suggest using the old-fashioned file folder system. You can get cardboard filing boxes and file folders inexpensively at any stationery store. Create a separate physical file for each category that you have in your Quicken or MS Money program and after you've entered the record electronically, simply dump the receipt in the physical file. Similarly, you can demand your physical checks back from your bank (for which they'll typically charge a nominal fee of a few dollars), use them to reconcile your electronic account, and then keep them in your file folder as well.

The beauty of this system is that once set up, you almost never need to go back and search through your physical files. The records are all kept electronically on your computer. Want to know whom you gave a check to on April 14th? Just punch in the appropriate keystrokes and you'll be told.

BUT, and it's a big but, if you ever do need the physical records, they are there, available to you in your physical file folder system. I never use more than one cardboard box a year for my physical system. I then write the year on the outside of the box, and store it in the garage, to be available if and when I ever need to establish a paper trail.

Paper and Electronics

Many people have openly embraced our modern world of computers and electronic files. I have, too. But only up to a point. I can assure you from bitter experience, however, that if you ever have an IRS audit, identity fraud, or challenge from a vendor who says you didn't pay them, having that paper trail is worth its weight in gold, even if it is old fashioned.

Now let's get back to those categories that you want to record.

TIP—NOT TAX
ADVICE

The information provided in this chapter is given to provide an overview. It is not intended as tax advice, nor should it be relied upon. If you need tax advice, obtain the services of a tax professional.

What Are Taxable Items?

As a new home owner, living in your home, you're probably going to be able to take some hefty deductions as part of your ownership. Many of these can be taken on an annual basis, although others, as we'll see shortly, must be saved long term for when you sell. The most common annual deductions are for property taxes and mortgage interest.

Property Taxes

Typically you are billed as part of your monthly mortgage payment. However, if you put more than 20 percent down when you purchased, you can opt to pay this yourself, directly. If you pay with your mortgage payment, your year-end statement from the lender will tell you how much you paid in taxes.

On the other hand, if you pay directly yourself, you usually have the choice of paying in two payments, which usually occur in December and April. You can, of course, pay them both at the same time on the first due date.

TIP—BILL NOTIFICATION

If you are running an electronic home record keeping program, as suggested above, you can easily set it to notify you when a tax bill is due, thus helping you to avoid late payment fees.

These property taxes are typically deductible from our federal and state income taxes, provided we itemize at the end of the year. Thus, if you pay directly yourself, you'll want to keep both a copy of the tax bill itself (it usually comes with a receipt for you to save), as well as your canceled check, which shows that you paid it as well as the date paid. (You can only deduct taxes in the year paid.)

Mortgage Interest

Most mortgage interest on your main residence is also deductible. The proof that you paid it is usually in a statement that comes to you at the end of the year (and hopefully before April 15th when your taxes are due), that tells you how much of your mortgage payment for the previous year went to interest and how much to principle.

TRAP—YOU CAN ONLY DEDUCT INTEREST

Don't make the mistake of thinking you can simply add up all your mortgage payments and take a deduction for that amount. Unless your mortgage is interest only, your payment is composed partly of interest and partly of principle. The principle is not deductible; the interest might be.

It's also a good idea to save each canceled check you send to your mortgage company. However, the IRS will probably accept the mortgage company's statement of how much interest you paid. You might just need the checks in case the mortgage company says you didn't make a payment. If your payments are automatically deducted from a bank account, be sure you save your bank statement showing the amount paid, to whom, and when.

TIP—THERE'S THE AMT FOR HIGHER-TAX-BRACKET OWNERS

 If you're a higher income earner, you might find that you qualify (lucky you) for the Alternative Minimum Tax. (Your accountant or your electronic tax preparation program should alert you to this.) If this is the case, you might find that you lose some of the deductions noted above.

As a home owner who occupies the property, you normally cannot deduct your costs for operating the home. This includes utilities, repairs, maintenance, depreciation, and so on. (The exception is when you have a home office, noted below.) These deductions can be taken only if your property is run as a business; that is, it's an investment and you rent it out to tenants. The tax code is tricky here, so if you're renting out your home, or a portion of it, be sure to check with your accountant.

Points

Generally speaking, some points (a percentage of the loan) that you pay to obtain a mortgage when you buy or refinance are deductible in the year you paid them. You must, however, have obtained the loan in connection with improving or purchasing your main (principal) residence and the mortgage must be secured by that home. (Also, the points cannot exceed the amount usually charged in your area.)

Thus, keep all the escrow and loan documents you receive when you buy or refinance. You might be able to make a sizable deduction for points.

On the other hand, if your accountant tells you that your loan points are not deductible in the year paid, you might be able to deduct them as paid each month over the term of the loan. For example, if the loan has 360 monthly payments, you might be able to divide the points by 360 and deduct 12 month's worth each year.

What Are Taxable Items for When I Sell?

When it comes time to sell your home, chances are you'll have made a substantial profit on it (assuming the market remains strong). If there is a gain, you might need to pay capital gains tax. (The exception would be if you qualify for the up to $500,000 for married couples filing jointly exclusion explained in Chapter 6.)

The question that now arises is just how big is your gain. Unless your know that, you won't know if you have any tax to pay.

Capital gain is calculated as the difference between your *adjusted tax basis* in the property and your *sales price*, less costs of sale. While the sales price is easily understood, the adjusted tax basis can cause some confusion.

What Is My Adjusted Tax Basis?

Your original tax basis is usually the cost of your home (or the cost to build it). It is "adjusted" by adding to it any improvements made and subtracting from it any depreciation, casualty losses, and a few other charges.

Tax Basis

- Original cost of property (including transaction costs)
- Plus improvement such as construction or remodeling
- Plus other capital improvements such as an assessment for adding a sewer
- Minus depreciation, casualty loss, or other loss

TIP—NO
DEPRECIATION

As a homeowner, you are not allowed to depreciate your property for tax purposes. However, you might be able to get a partial depreciation deduction IF you have a home office. See below.

Here's an example:

You buy a home for $250,000 (including transaction costs) and that becomes your tax basis. After living in the property for a year, you find that you need additional room, so you add an extra bedroom at a cost of $50,000. Now, your tax basis is adjusted (bumped up) to $300,000.

Two years later you sell for $400,000 (including transaction costs). What is your capital gain?

Your gain is the difference between your adjusted basis and your sales price. Originally your basis was $250,000. However, because you added a room, you adjusted your basis up to the $300,000 so your gain is $100,000. Note, if you had not added the room, your gain would have been $50,000 more, or $150,000.

Naturally, the smaller your taxable gain, the smaller your tax will be. At a 15-percent capital gain rate, the savings between $150,000 and $100,000 in our example is $7500. Thus, it's certainly to your advantage to have a higher basis than a lower one. But, in order to have that higher basis, you're going to need to document the fact that it cost $50,000 to add that additional room. Therefore, records you will want to keep include:

- Canceled checks for materials and labor
- Bills from contractors
- Paid receipts

You'll want to keep your documentation until you sell your home so that you can prove that you spent what you said you spent.

TRAP—KEEP
YOUR RECORDS!

Many people suggest keeping your documentation, your paper trail, only for three or four years and keeping your tax returns for at least 10 years. My feeling is that as a homeowner, you need to keep all of your documentation, your entire paper trail, as long as you own the home, and for many years afterward. I recently had to dig up an 11-year-old professional inspection report for a home I was selling. Fortunately, I had kept the records in a filing box.

Thus, as a homeowner, you'll want to keep receipts and records of all of the items that you paid for that improve your property. In this way you can adjust your tax basis upward and lower your capital gain.

Improvement versus Repair/Maintenance

It's important to understand that everything you spend on your home is not necessarily an improvement. For example, if your gas water heater goes out and you replace it with a similar gas water heater, you haven't really improved your property. You've simply repaired or maintained it. Thus, the new gas water heater probably would not count toward adjusting your tax basis upward.

On the other hand, if instead of simply replacing the old gas water heater, you instead put in an expensive solar heating system, you might have improved your property and part of the cost of the solar water system might be considered an improvement that would adjust your tax basis upward. Be sure to check with your accountant for specific items to see if they might be considered repairs/maintenance, or actual improvements to your property. You'll want to keep records of improvements far longer than records of repairs.

TRAP—NO DEDUCTION FOR A LOSS

If you are unfortunate enough to sell during the down cycle of the real estate market, you might find that you're selling your home for a tax loss. Unfortunately, as of this writing, you cannot take a tax loss on a personal residence. It's a quirk of the tax code.

Should I Keep General Receipts?

Generally speaking, I keep all my receipts, as well as proof of payment, for everything I buy (excluding items which are tax deductible) for at least as long as the return or charge period. For example, I recently bought some bare root plants for the back yard. They have a six-month warranty. (If they don't grow, I can return them.) I kept my receipt and returned one that didn't grow.

Similarly, any receipts for charges I make on credit cards I keep at least at least until the charge comes through on my monthly statement. (Of course, I keep it much longer if it has to do with a home improvement, as noted above, or for a home office, noted below.)

Should I Keep Utility Bill Receipts?

Generally speaking, you cannot take a deduction for your utility bills. The exception here is when you have a home office (see below).

However, some homeowners do keep accurate records of their utility costs in order see how much it's costing them to live in the property. This is especially important for those on fixed incomes. By tracking your monthly utility bills, you can sometimes make adjustments (adjusting the thermostat cooler in winter, hotter in summer) to keep those bills from getting too high. Also, tracking utility costs from year-to-year can let you know if you're starting to live a bit too excessively for your means. Unless I have a home office, I generally keep my utility bill receipts for only a year.

What if I Have a Home Office?

If you have your own business, you might be able to designate a portion of your home as your office. If you do, then the rules for business deductions apply to that space. Note: The home office rules are tricky and seem to change frequently. The following is an overview, but be sure to check with your accountant regarding your own situation.

TRAP—STRICTLY FOLLOWED

The IRS demands that the home office rules be strictly observed. Otherwise, almost anyone could claim a home office.

Qualifying as a Home Office

- You must have your own business. If you are an employee using a home office, special limiting rules apply. See your accountant.
- The office must be your principal place of business or it must be where you meet clients or customers or hold business meetings in the course of doing business. (No other outside location exists for doing business.)
- You must use it regularly, not occasionally.
- You must use it exclusively for business purposes.

This last is often confusing to homeowners running a business. For example, you might use the dining room table to conduct business. But, you also use it for dining. This area would *not* qualify as it is not used *solely* for business purposes. On the other hand, if you designate a specific room, say a bedroom, or even a portion of a room, say an alcove that is used exclusively for business and for nothing else, then it should qualify.

TIP—EXCEPTIONS AND SPECIAL SITUATIONS

Special exceptions exist for when a portion of the home is used for day care, storage of goods, and so on. Check with your accountant.

TRAP—BUSINESS ACTIVITY

You must have an *active*, not *passive* business. This excludes an office for tracking your personal stock investments, for example.

Home Office Deductions

If you qualify for a home office, you can generally take the business deductions only for that portion of your home used as the office. For example, if your home has 2000 square feet and you are using one bedroom of 100 square feet as your office, you could take 1/20th of your home expenses as a deduction. If your overall expenses were $10,000 annually, in our example above you could take 1/20th of that or $500 as a deduction.

General Deductions Allowed for a Home Office

- Property taxes
- Mortgage interest
- Depreciation
- Insurance
- Maintenance
- Repairs
- Utilities
- Other costs associated with the business operation

The advantage of the home office deduction is that you get a deduction for the expenses of the home office from your income taxes. Thus, your home helps offset the taxes you pay.

What Happens When I Sell?

Again, this is an area where the rules seem to change frequently, so check with your accountant. Generally speaking, when you sell and you use the up-to-$500,000 exclusion on a personal residence (see Chapter 6), the home office does not create a special gain. In other words, you do not have to pay a separate capital gain tax on the portion of your home used as an office.

However, you might have to pay tax on the recapture of depreciation. If you took depreciation as an expense while you used your home office, the amount taken might come back and need to be taxed. As I said, it's tricky and tends to change often, so see your accountant.

Record Keeping

You'll want to keep accurate records of all your home office expenses—including utilities, all repairs, and maintenance—so that you can take a percentage of them as a deduction for your home office. As with all tax records, I would save them indefinitely.

TRAP—TAX RECORDS

As noted earlier, you are often advised to save records for tax purposes for only three or four years. Personally, I save them indefinitely. The reason is that the tax rules change. At some time in the future, you might discover (for whatever reason) that you under-paid or overdeducted to the point where it technically constitutes fraud. In that case the IRS might challenge your records going back a decade or more, depending on the rules at the time. Having an accurate paper trail can help enormously if that happens.

6

Tax Planning for When You Sell

Once again, it might seem incongruous to think about selling your property as soon as you've bought it. However, careful tax planning can help ensure that when you do sell, assuming you make a profit, you won't have a big tax bill to worry about.

TIP—NOT TAX ADVICE

 The tax information provided in this book is given to provide an overview. It is not intended as advice nor should it be relied upon. If you need tax advice, obtain the services of a tax professional.

Much of the tax planning for a sale of a personal residence these days revolves around being sure that you qualify for the up-to-$500,000 exclusion (for married couples filing jointly) provided for under the 1997 Taxpayer Relief Act. That's what we'll cover in this chapter. According to this Act, each person, regardless of age, can exclude up to $250,000 of the capital gain on a principle residence. For a couple, that adds up to $500,000 when they file a joint return.

Obviously, being able to exclude up to $500,000 of the gain can make a huge difference in your tax liability. And for most people, it's a highly desirable option. (I say "most" because for some wealthy taxpayers whose gain is substantially more than the maximum, other alternatives, such as converting to a rental and subsequently doing a tax-deferred exchange might be an option.)

There are some basic rules that must be followed in order to qualify for the exclusion:

Basic Exclusion Rules

- The home must be your principal residence—you must own and occupy it.
- You must have lived in the property for 2 out of the previous 5 years.
- You can only take the exclusion once every 2 years.

While the basics are fairly simple, there are many circumstances that come close, but do not quite fit the formula. Before considering these, however, let's take a quick look at what this law changed.

Old Rules No Longer in Effect

There were many tax planning rules prior to the change in the tax code, and unfortunately many people still think they apply. Here are some that are no longer applicable:

No Rollover

In the past, you had to purchase another property of the same or greater value in order to defer gain. At that time it was not an *exclusion* but a *deferral.* Your gain was deferred into the future and into the new property.

Today, that's no longer the case. You do not have to buy another property at any time nor defer the gain into it.

No Need to Reinvest in Property

Further, the money that you take out of the property need not be reinvested in another property. You can do with it as you wish, take a holiday, gamble it away in Vegas, or give it to your children.

No Age Requirement

In the past the rule applied only if you were aged 55 or older. That provision has been repealed. You do not need to reach a minimum age in order to qualify.

No Move Away Requirement

You do not have to move a certain distance, for example 50 miles, away from your old home in order to qualify for the exclusion.

Previously Used "Once in a Lifetime Exclusion"

The fact that you previously took the exclusion under the old rules in no way precludes you from taking it again under the new rules. In effect, you get it back.

No Form 2119

In the past the home sale had to be reported on form 2119. That was eliminated a year after the new rules took effect. See the end of this chapter for more information on reporting requirements.

New Rules Are Specific

To qualify, the house must be your principal residence. That means that it must be your "main house." Often it means simply where you spend a majority of your time. If you have two houses (a second vacation home, for example) your principal residence is often determined by many factors including:

Determining If It's Your Principal Residence

- Where your family resides
- Near where you work
- The address you use when sending in your federal and state tax returns
- Your mailing address for bills
- Where you are registered to vote
- Other factors indicating you live there

You must also live in it for a minimum of two out of five years. That means that if you moved in yesterday, it will be two years before you can claim the exclusion. (There are some extenuating circumstances, which we'll discuss shortly.)

From a tax-planning standpoint, assuming you make a profit on your house, it's therefore likely to be to your advantage to remain in the home at least two years before selling it.

What if I Rent Out My House?

While you might plan on residing in your home right now, your circumstances might change in the future. You might find that you need to move away because of a job change, change in your marital situation or health, or for any number of other reasons. Rather than sell the property, you might opt to rent it out. Will renting it preclude claiming the exclusion?

TRAP—THE IRS MIGHT DISAGREE WITH YOU

Over the years there have been a wide variety of rulings from the IRS on what constitutes occupancy. This has been particularly contentious when a second or even a third vacation home have been involved. Be sure you check with your accountant for the current thinking on the matter.

No, provided you meet the time guidelines. Remember, you must have resided in the property for two out of the previous five years. That means that you can rent the property out for three out of the previous five years. Furthermore, the periods of occupancy and renting do not have to be continuous. You could live in it for year, rent it out for three years, and then come back and live in it for one year, thus meeting the requirement.

What If I Take Extended Vacations?

It depends on the circumstances. For example, you take a cruise that lasts a few months. This is a temporary vacation and probably won't affect your occupancy status with regard to the home.

On the other hand, you take a 15-month leave of absence from work and move to another country during that time, even though you did not rent out the home. This will probably be construed as time when you did not occupy the property.

TIP—KEEP THE DATES ACCURATELY

You don't want to miss the two-out-of-five-year rule because you were off a few days. If you're not sure, err on the side of a few more days than two years. Generally speaking, the time periods begin when title transfers to you and ends when title actually transfers to another owner.

What If Two Unmarried People Own the House?

Then each one must independently qualify for the maximum limitation. Each will file separate returns, report the gains, and may claim up to the $250,000 exclusion per person.

What If Only One Spouse Qualifies?

This opens a whole can of worms. For example, it is possible for each spouse to have his or her separate principal residence. If that's the case, then each could potentially qualify for the up-to-$250,000 exclusion on their properties, provided they meet the basic requirements.

Or, if both spouses own the property, but only one has occupied it for two years (as when there is a marriage and one member previously owned the house), then only the spouse who has occupied it for two years may claim the exclusion.

Exceptions to the Rule

Even though you fully intend to meet the guidelines of the exclusion rule, circumstances might prevent you from doing so. If that's the case, then you might still be able to claim at least a part of the up to $500,000 (for married couples filing jointly), if not all, of the amount.

Change in Health

You might contract an illness or have an accident that necessitates your moving from the house. For example, you are in a car accident and lose the use of your legs. Your current home has many stairs, so you sell it in order to acquire a home that's all on one level.

Change in Employment

You lose your current job and find another one across the state or the country. Generally the move must be for more than 50 miles. Hence, you are forced to sell your home.

Other Unforeseen Events

These must meet the scrutiny of the IRS. Generally speaking you will need to establish that the primary reason for the sale was unanticipated. This is usually on a case-by-case basis but might include condemnation of the house or breakup of a couple that intended to get married.

TIP—THERE ARE MANY EXCEPTIONS

Don't assume that you must be transferred more than 50 miles away to benefit from the exclusion if you haven't occupied the property for two years. For example, you might be relying on a mass transit system to get you to work, but for some reason the city closes down the line you're on. Now you can't get to work. You might claim that because of this you were forced to sell and move. Or perhaps it isn't your health, but that of your spouse or a family member that's changed and forced your move. Be sure to check with your accountant to see if your special circumstances might qualify.

How Much, if Any, of the Exclusion Do I Get?

If you have a qualified exception, then you might get at least a partial exclusion. Generally speaking this is determined by one of two formulas. Either you divide the days of use into two years (730 days) or the days between the sale of your last home which qualified for the exclusion and the current sale into two years. Whichever is less is taken as a percentage, which then applies to the up to $500,000 exclusion for a couple filing jointly. If, for example, you had a qualified exception, hadn't previously taken the exclusion, and you occupied your principal residence for six months, you would probably end up with one-fourth of the exclusion amount.

How Do I Report the Exclusion?

Generally speaking, if your gain does not exceed the $250,000 per person or $500,000 per married couple filing jointly, you do not need to report the sale. If the gain exceeds these amounts, then you need to report it on schedule 1040, Schedule D to the federal government and as your state requires.

What about the Records I've Been Keeping?

If your gain is not going to exceed $250,000 for individuals or $500,000 for couples filing jointly, then there's really no need to keep records of expenses that affect your basis as noted in the previous chapters, because you won't have any capital gains taxes to pay.

However, most people have no idea what their gain is going to be. Homes purchased as little as five years ago in some areas of the country have doubled and even tripled in value. Therefore, to be safe, as noted in the last chapter, I suggest that you do keep records that will affect the basis of your property. Who knows? When it comes time to sell, you might find that your gain is more than the $250,000 for individuals or $500,000 limit for married couples filing jointly and you would have tax to pay on the excess. However, if you've kept adequate records and your basis is adjusted upwards, you might find that tax is reduced—or even eliminated.

7

Security for
Your Home

Security, for the home and the nation, was underscored by the terrible events of 9/11. Today as never before, no one in America underestimates the need for security.

However, it's probably unrealistic to worry about a terrorist attack on your home. Terrorists seem to want highly visible public targets. If your home is physically attacked at all, the most likely attackers are going to be burglars looking for financial gain. Further down the list are likely to be rapists, arsonists, or murderers.

In point of fact, the most likely source of attack on your home isn't going to come from someone physically breaking in at all, but rather from a crook attempting to steal your financial secrets and use them for his or her personal gain—identity theft. (We'll cover this at the end of the chapter.) That doesn't mean that someone won't break in—they might.

A new home owner is sure to wonder if he or she needs protection. And if so, how much and what kind? Or perhaps you already have some protection. When you bought your home, maybe you found a security system with a few magnetic window and door sensors and a couple of heat/motion detectors in place. Maybe you're thinking this is all the security you need. Maybe not.

In this chapter we'll look at some of the different ways of protecting your home. First we'll deal with physical measures to protect your home from brute force. Later in the chapter we'll delve into electronic countermeasures.

How Secure Is Your Neighborhood?

Before even thinking about putting home security measures into place, I suggest you do the following exercise (if you didn't do it before making your purchase). Go to your local police station, the one closest to your home, and talk to the public affairs officer (or whoever happens to be handling public relations). Ask to see the crime statistics for your block.

It's often a surprise to learn that most police agencies keep detailed statistics not only for citywide crime, but also for crimes committed within neighborhoods and even by block. While you might not get a list of who committed the crime, you should be able to get a list of how many home break-ins, auto thefts, rapes, and so on were committed over the last year and sometimes going back decades. In this way you can quickly gain a very accurate estimate of what the crime scene is like in your neighborhood.

**TIP—THE PAST
ONLY SUGGESTS
THE FUTURE**

Crimes committed on your street in the past are not perfect indicators. However, a lot of past crimes do suggest that more will be committed in the future.

If it turns out that there have been a significant number (usually more than one in a year is a significant number) of home break-ins that happened in your area, you might want to take aggressive precautions against a physical assault on your home. On the other hand, if there have been very few home break-ins, you might feel more secure with a less aggressive approach. We'll consider a variety of home security measures from the most aggressive to the least.

Physically Protecting Your Home

Most home break-ins occur when the occupant is out. The burglar "cases" the house to be sure that you're away, then typically breaks in and quickly steals whatever valuables happen to be easily accessed. Much more serious are home break-ins when the occupant is present, because these can lead to physical assaults.

The most common response when a home break-in occurs in a neighborhood that has previously been relatively crime-free, is for homeowners to create a "fortress house." The idea is to physically stop intruders. This can be more or less successful, or desirable, depending on the approach.

Window/Door Bars

This is often considered the ultimate home protection by people who live in high crime areas. There are always companies (check the Yellow Pages of your phone book) who are eager to install these on your home.

Barring up your house does make it more difficult for the "spontaneous" criminal, the one who picks a house at random, to burglarize. It's not clear, however, that bars will keep away a truly determined assault on your home.

Barring your house, however, does carry with it at least two concerns. The first is appearance. If you ever hope to sell your home, having bars on the doors and windows, no matter how attractive they might be, is a sure turnoff to buyers. Buyers will immediately assume, perhaps correctly, that yours is a high-crime area and will look elsewhere. In order to sell, you might have to accept a lower price.

**TRAP—IT'S THE
NEIGHBORHOOD
APPEARANCE
THAT COUNTS**

Even if you don't have bars on your windows and doors, if your neighbors do, it tells the same story to would-be buyers. Yours is an unsafe place to live.

The second problem has to do with your personal safety. There have been countless stories of people who have burned up in home fires because they couldn't get out through barred doors and windows. It's important to remember that both doors and windows are portals, routes of egress from your home in an emergency. (Most building departments, in fact, insist that all bedrooms have windows built at least a minimum size in order to allow occupants to quickly break them out and escape in case of fire.) For this reason, some building departments will not allow windows and doors to be barred. Or if they do, the bars must have devices that allow them to be quickly retracted.

If you're considering barring up your house, don't just look at it from the perspective of someone trying to get in. Also consider how difficult it might be if you need to get out.

Window/Door Locks

A lesser level of protection, although one that's possibly more realistic for most people, is to "harden" your home through adding more secure locking systems. Criminals often scoff at the way most homes are so easily accessed. Most doors and windows can be quickly jimmied open.

I had this experience myself a few years ago. I had a second home in an isolated area. I drove to it one day (it was a good 11 hours from my other home), only to find I had forgotten the front door keys. I couldn't get in through any windows (not knowing how to jimmy them) and didn't want to break one because of the replacement cost. However, I knew I could get a new door handle/lock for under 20 bucks. So I determined to break my way in there.

I had a hammer in my car and figured I would smash away at the existing door handle/lock until it finally gave way. Hopefully, I wouldn't damage the door in the process. Imagine my surprise when at the first slight blow of the hammer, the handle flew off, the lock disintegrated, and the door swung open! My front door lock was actually offering little to no security at all.

The moral here is that many homes come equipped with relatively unsecure locks. Today, when you go to Home Depot, Lowes, or other building supply stores, you can buy locks for your doors that are rated in terms of their security factor. You might need to pay a hundred dollars, but get one with a high security rating—today you can buy a lock that will stop a sledge hammer!

My suggestion is that you put a good lock, including a deadbolt, on all your exterior doors. Keep in mind that most exterior doors are solid core. That means that unlike interior doors, which are often hollow, exterior doors are filled with either wood or some other material. This makes them very difficult to break through. (It also often provides some fire protection as well.) Put a good lock on a solid-core door and it becomes much more difficult for someone to break into your home.

Windows should also have two separate locking systems. The first is a lock that secures the movable portion of the window to the fixed portion. However, because this can often be easily jimmied, a second lock that keeps the window from physically being opened offers added protection. Modern windows usually come with a plug, dowel, or other device for securing the window. If your home doesn't have this, then you can buy simple screw-on devices at a hardware store that will serve the same purpose. Sometimes simply putting a stick behind a sliding window will prohibit it from begin opened.

TIP—LOCKS DON'T PREVENT BREAKAGE

Of course, a burglar could always break the window. However, this is less likely to happen because of the noise it causes and the fact that someone is likely to see this and call the cops.

TRAP—ELECTRONIC SENSORS MIGHT NOT DETECT BROKEN WINDOWS

Many of the magnetic window sensors available as home protection devices in the past only detected when a window was opened, not when it was broken. It's something to consider when paying a lot of money for electronic protection. Better modern window sensors detect the sound of glass breaking or the loss of integrity of the window.

Neighborhood Watch Programs

Beyond physically securing your home with bars and locks, perhaps the most effective system for deterring break-ins is also the least costly. It simply gets your neighborhood involved in a program to watch out for criminal activity.

As noted, most home break-ins occur when no one is around, so whenever I'm going to be gone for more than a day or two, I alert my neighbors to this fact. I simply give them a call, email them, or knock on their doors and mention that I'll be out of town and give them the dates. I ask them if they'll keep a lookout on the house. (Of course, you need to trust your neighbors to do this!)

Most neighbors are very sensitive to security. They want their neighborhood to be as safe as possible. They almost form a kind of clan or pack mentality and will go out of their way to protect your property while you're gone. In my case they will take in newspapers and flyers that get left so that my house doesn't look abandoned. If a box should be delivered and left at the front door, they'll hold it for me. They'll even take in mail that gets stuffed into my mailbox.

Your neighbors might not be as conscientious. Or they might be even more so. However, having neighbors watch out for your home while you're away (or even when you're there) to my way of thinking is probably the best security you can find.

All of which is why I suggest that if your neighborhood hasn't done so, you should help organize a neighborhood watch program. This is easily done by contacting your local police department. A specific person will usually be designated for each block (usually the neighborhood busybody is best), and everyone will have information passed out to them on what to watch out for and the correct numbers to call in case of emergencies. Plus, neighborhood watch signs will be posted, alerting criminals to the fact that your neighborhood is on alert. Statistics suggest that this program does help prevent neighborhood crime.

Security Companies

In addition to the above basically passive systems, there are also many security companies that offer on-site protection. These companies typically will have their own patrol cars that will come by on a regular or occasional basis and check out your house. They also might install electronic security devices that will alert them and/or the police to intrusions and cause them to send a car racing to your home.

While these can be among the most effective deterrents to crime, they can also be among the most expensive. If you're interested in this level of security, then I suggest you check into the Internet using the following keywords: home security companies. You should find a host of offerings.

Electronic Protection

In today's world, electronic home protection is the rage. Indeed, it does offer an enormous amount of sophisticated technology that will help secure your home. However, it's important to understand that just because it's electronic, that doesn't mean it will perform miracles. If you simply leave your doors or windows unlocked, or don't set your security system, you're not likely to avoid sustaining a loss if you have a robbery.

There are many kinds of electronic home security systems available today (see the reference section at the end of this chapter). These include the following:

Electronic Home Security Measures

- Door/window magnetic, audio, and integrity sensors
- Heat/motion/sound detectors
- Alarm bells
- Call systems that alert police or a security company
- Video/audio surveillance

Whole House Systems

Whole house electronic security systems have been around for decades. Typically a company will come in and install sensors on all your exterior doors and windows. Usually one or two (or perhaps more) motion/heat/sound detectors will be placed at critical junctures in your house. Often they are mounted high up where they are less obvious and aim at entranceways or large open areas. These will be linked either by wires or by wireless means to a central command post. This is essentially a small computer that receives input.

TRAP—BE WARY OF SECURITY SELLERS

Sometimes when a security company contacts you, you'll be asked to fill out information so that they can come to your home and give you a free inspection and evaluation. Be aware of whom you're giving information to and letting into your house. It could be the crooks! Also, be careful of buying from salespeople who might be making a hefty commission by getting you to buy the biggest, most expensive system.

The system typically will be inactive until armed. You can arm it by keying in a code (also the way to disarm it) or sometimes by simply setting up an electronic clock that tells it when to go on or off.

If it detects an intrusion into your home, it can do a variety of things, depending on the sophistication of the system and what you've programmed in. These include:

- Setting off a loud klaxon to scare aware intruders and alert neighbors of a problem.
- Issuing a loud warning inside the home that, hopefully, will scare aware intruders.
- Silently making a phone call to a security company that can then either send out its own patrol car or alert police.
- Calling the local police department and letting them know that they need to investigate.
- Calling you on your cell phone and alerting you to the problem.

Companies that install these whole home security systems usually swear by their effectiveness. However, having known a good many people who have had them, it seems they also come with potential problems (see below).

Advantages of Whole Home Security Systems

- They can be "on" continuously and provide security 24/7.
- They can detect the most common kinds of home break-ins.
- When connected to a phone, they can call for human backup.
- A sign posted in front of your home alerting would-be burglars that the system is in place can be a strong deterrent.
- They can have battery backup in case the power is out.

On the other hand, these whole home systems are not foolproof, and they do have drawbacks. When I was a teenager, a good many years ago, I was fascinated both by electronics and home security. Having much spare time, I designed a primitive electronic system. When a door or window was opened, two electrical contacts would meet and an alarm would be sounded. The alarm would show up both as a bell ringing and as a light flashing on a board showing where the break-in had occurred.

You can imagine my delight in showing this working system off to my parents. You can also imagine my chagrin when a neighborhood chum happened by during my demonstration, saw it in operation, and quickly defeated it by taking a leaf from a tree and putting it between the two contacts, thus immediately shutting off the system.

TIP—X10 SYSTEMS ARE POPULAR

This deals with the question of how to set up a security system in a home that's not already wired for it. Rewiring is very costly, messy, and often looks bad. Wireless systems can be expensive. However, X10 systems use the existing electrical wiring of your home to transmit electronic signals. The sending/receiving units are relatively inexpensive. Yes, they do work. Although they can be defeated if, for example, you happen to have an electric motor as from a hair dryer turned on, if they are on the other side of a transformer, or if the would-be burglar cuts the power to your home.

The moral of this story is not that today's modern whole house systems are so unsophisticated that they can be defeated by a leaf or the foil wrapper from a stick of gum (which could, indeed, defeat some of the earlier systems). Rather, it's that no system is foolproof and criminals are getting increasingly sophisticated.

For example, some systems rely on magnetic sensors. When a door or window is opened, the contact is broken and the alarm sounded. Some of these, however, will not sound an alarm if a burglar breaks a portion of the window but does not move the frame or disturb the contacts. And others can be defeated by using a wire extension to complete the circuit while the window is opened.

Of course, more sophisticated systems will set off the alarm if the window is broken or if any attempt is made to mess with the electronics of the system. But, then again, even more sophisticated criminals undoubtedly have means around these countermeasures.

**TIP—YOU WANT
TO DISCOURAGE
ATTEMPTED
BREAK-INS**

The whole point of whole house systems is not to guarantee security, but to discourage criminals. If your house has a system and another one doesn't, which one is it going to be easier for the burglar to attack?

**Problems with
Whole Home Systems**

- They tend to be expensive, often costing into the thousands of dollars for a complete installation, which can include battery back-up and cell phone activation.

- They can be annoying if they go off by accident. Perhaps you forgot to inactivate the system, or a friend or relative comes in unexpectedly and the alarm goes off.

- The police department will not necessarily be happy that you have the systems. False alarms, caused by people accidentally tripping the system, wastes police resources. Some departments have taken to charging as much as $500 for each time they respond to a false alarm.

- Most alarm systems require that you arm them and you might forget. Or it might simply become too much of a bother to do so. Hence, the system becomes ineffective.

- They are not 100 percent foolproof.

Video/Audio Surveillance Systems

Now we come to my personal favorite. These systems rely on microphones and video cameras and, best of all, they can easily be set up by any home computer hobbyist (although companies abound that will set them up for you).

If you already have a computer, perhaps you've been introduced to the world of webcams. These are video cameras that are typically placed on top of your computer facing you. They take continuous images.

Using appropriate software that's simple to install and operate, you can take the video signal from the webcam into your computer and using an Internet connection, send it to another computer anywhere in the world. Thus, two people who are appropriately outfitted with webcams, software, computers, and an Internet connection can see each other in real time. Additionally, a microphone can be connected to the webcam, which will then transmit not only video, but audio feed as well.

Today there are webcams operating 24/7 around the world. Try a search engine using the word, "Webcam." You can use your Internet access program—Explorer, Netscape, and so on—to easily access these and see continuous views of the Eiffel Tower, the Golden Gate Bridge, or whatever someone happens to be putting up at the time.

The applications of this for home security should be obvious. Webcams (which can be purchased for under $30) can be situated at critical points in and around your home. They can be connected by wires (or can be wireless, although the cost is increased) to send the A/V signal to your computer.

Your computer can be connected to the Internet and can broadcast a continuous signal to another computer anywhere in the world, which can then look in and listen to your home. Alternatively, this system can be connected to a variety of sensors around the home, which activate it only when there is an intrusion.

Thus you can be alerted when there is movement in your home. You can actually see what's happening. And then you can take appropriate action.

TIP—YOU DON'T NEED LIGHT

Most webcams operate on visible light. Hence, they are blind at night. However, you can use sensors that will turn on the lights when motion is sensed. Or you can use infrared webcams (and infrared illuminators) that don't need any visible light at all.

Advantages of A/V Surveillance Systems

- You can see and hear what's happening at your home, even when you're far away.

- If you already have a computer and Internet access, they can be inexpensive to install.

- You can do it yourself.

Sound too good to be true? Well, of course it is. I set up a system such as this recently between my vacation cabin and my regular home. And it worked pretty well most of the time. But it was easily defeated, and not necessarily by burglars.

For example, I use a DSL line for high-speed broadband access. However, at my cabin's location, the DSL line seems to be down more than it's up due to problems with the provider. Whenever it's down, my surveillance is also down. (I have a cable-modem at my regular home and it's not much more reliable.)

Also, power outages can easily take out the system. And any possible burglar can simply cover up the camera and mike, thus eliminating the surveillance, although this in itself can be an alert.

Problems with
A/V Surveillance Systems

- They depend on a constant Internet connection, which can frequently be down and is expensive to maintain.

- Your computer must be on all the time—computer glitches might take down the surveillance.

- You or someone must monitor the system (unless you pay for a security company), and you're likely to often be unavailable.

TRAP—YOUR COM- PUTER MIGHT BE VULNERABLE

Any computer that's online all the time is subject to invasion from hackers. While they just might want to see what you're watching, they also might have thievery on their minds. A good firewall, updated operating system, and virus/spy protection will help.

A/V System and Security Company

For what is usually a substantial amount of money, many security companies will outfit your home with A/V surveillance to their offices. Instead of your watching, they watch. If there's a problem they can send out their own cars—or notify the police.

Additional Applications

It's worth noting that one additional application of an A/V surveillance system can be for monitoring someone such as a baby or elderly person. These can be set up around the house. Additionally, there are personal systems now available for the elderly that have an alert system located conveniently in the house, or strapped to a wrist for example, that will alert a security system or automatically call a relative.

Identity Theft

You might wonder why I've included this in a chapter on home security. However, my reasoning should quickly become evident. For most of us, our home is also our family office, the place where we conduct all of our family's financial business. That means that we have loads of sensitive documents constantly going into and coming out of our house.

A decade or two ago, this was no problem. The mails were considered inviolate, as was our garbage. That's no longer the case. A friend of mine recently had some checks stolen right out of his mailbox. These checks were issued by his bank as part of a promotion hoping to entice him to use his home equity line of credit.

The thieves knew his address, bank, and account number, and his social security number, which he surmises they got by going through his garbage and finding it listed on a medical statement he had thrown out. (Medical statements often use social security numbers to identify you to their plans.) The thieves called his bank and pretended to be him. They got his bank to change his address to one across the country and to send them new checks, which they promptly cashed. His loss was $102,000, which the bank eventually made good.

The moral here is that home security does not simply involve someone breaking into the house. They could also break into your mail and even your garbage.

While I don't believe there's any way to protect yourself completely here, it would suggest at minimum that you get a paper shredder and shred all documents that contain your name and address and other important information. No, it's not crazy and it's not paranoid, given the world in which we live with its sophisticated thieves.

I also suggest you call your bank and encourage them not to send out any checks to you that you don't authorize. Also, check all bank statements closely and immediately. And it wouldn't hurt to once a week call your bank or check online to make sure your account hasn't been tampered with.

Resources

Brinkshomesecurity.com—Security services

Cert.org/homeusers/homecomputerservices.com—From Carnegie Mellon, information on protecting your home computer

Circuitcity.com—Sells security devices

Easyhome security.com—Wireless systems

Frys.com—Sells security devices

Google.com—The best online search engine I've ever found

inetcam.com—iVISTA Personal Security system—A good place to start looking

Safety4life.com—GE security systems

Smarthome.com—Educational information and sells security systems

televiewersystems.com—Lets you use your own camcorder for surveillance

trackercam.com—Provides sophisticated robotic control for surveillance cameras

8

Did You Pay
Too Much?

Everyone these days seems to be playing the money game with their homes. It's a kind of guessing game that's popular at parties, over coffee when reading about home prices in the newspaper, and when talking about net worth with your financial advisor.

The money game is a guessing contest in which you try to estimate the true value of your home. With prices in many areas of the country accelerating over the past few years, most people love to play. It's fun to sit around and guesstimate how much your home has gone up in value. You bought it for $175,000 or $350,000 or whatever and now it's worth 35 percent more. Or is really worth 50 percent more? Could it actually have doubled in value over the past four years?! (The money game doesn't play nearly so well in a down market.)

Knowing the current value of your home is important for a variety of reasons, not the least of which is to give you, the owner, some piece of mind. Here are some other reasons why it's important to know your home's value:

Reasons to Know What Your Home is Currently Worth

- So you can determine your equity position
- So you can determine how much cash you can pull out in a sale or refi caused by an emergency
- So you can determine your net worth (given that homes now contribute a significant portion for most people)
- So you can determine how well, or badly, you've done in the r market.

- So you can get a handle on how good, or bad, your neighborhood is becoming (neighborhoods are what give homes most of their value)
- So you can determine how much, if any, money you can afford to put into your home in improvements

Do You Know Your Home's Current Value?

Most people read the newspaper and guesstimate their home's value based on articles that talk about values. Typically these give percentage price increases (or decreases) by zip code. For example, 91361 might have shown a price increase of 10 percent over the past six months, ergo you believe your home is now worth 10 percent more than it was.

Another method that's commonly used is based on recent neighborhood sales. A house up the street sold for $450,000. Therefore, you believe your home is worth $450,000.

Or a real estate agent will send out a flyer that says something like, "Homes in your area have gone up 15 percent in value—want to cash yours in?—List with ...." Or you might have just bought and moved into your home. So your assessment is that your home is worth exactly what you paid for it.

All of these are, indeed, somewhat valid measurements. If nothing else, they tend to give you the trend in values for your area, or at least a recent spot price. However, they are not really a highly accurate method of determining the true value of your home at any given time. Let's look at each separately:

Reports of Price Increases

These are typically compiled from sales figures and are for a fairly large geographical area, perhaps an entire city or zip code. The problem here is that within any area there are going to be prices that are higher as well as lower, often by significant amounts. Yes, your zip code might indeed have gone up by 7 percent or 11 percent or whatever, but your specific house could conceivably have gone down by 3 percent—or up by 20 percent. Geographical price increases show trends, but not specifics.

Nearby Sales

The tendency is to assume that whatever the nearby home sold for is the price of your home. (Many owners add a bit because they know their homes are better!)

The problem, however, is that the nearby home might or might not be similar to yours. It could have more or less square footage. It could be in better or worse shape. It could have a more or less attractive location and appearance, and so on.

Further, you don't usually know the conditions of the sale. Did the sellers find a buyer who fell in love with the place and paid more than top dollar? Or were they forced to sell quickly at a lower price because of a forced job change, illness, divorce, or other pressure situation?

Finally, do you really know the sales price? Too often neighborhood gossip will exaggerate the price. Unless you get it from an agent who's taking it right from reported sales (or from the country assessor's or recorder's office), the price you hear might not be accurate. Nearby sales can sometimes do more harm than good by providing a false price base for your home.

Flyers from Agents

Again, these usually reflect price trends based on recent sales in your geographical area. However, they normally aren't specific to your home. Unless the agent comes out and gives you a complete analysis just for your home, the flyers tend mostly to provide hope, not necessarily pricing reality.

Your Recent Purchase Price

What could be more accurate than the recent sale of the very home you're in to determine price? You paid $325,000 for your home, hence that definitively establishes its value, right?

Not necessarily. You could have paid too much. Or maybe you got a bargain and paid far under market.

Further, just because you paid $325,000, that doesn't mean you can net that much if you sell. Assuming you could get the same price, there are still transaction costs. A real estate commission to an agent could be 6 percent. Add in other closing costs and the total could cost you 8 to 10 percent in fees to sell your house. Assuming 10 percent, your NET is only $292,500. That's if you want to sell it the day you move in and can get the same price you bought for.

TRAP—DON'T OVER-LOOK TRANSACTION COSTS

They say that the minute you drive a new car off the dealer's lot, it loses 10 percent or more in value. The same happens the minute you buy your home, not because it's gone down in price, but because it will cost you about that much in transaction fees in order to sell it.

All of which is to say that most of the methods we use to determine what our house is worth at any given time are at best only approximations. At worst, they could be miles off.

So how do you determine the actual value of your home at any given time? Perhaps more important to many owners, how do you determine what it's like to be worth in the future 3, 5, 7, 10, or 15 years down the road? That's what we'll look into in this chapter.

CMA—Comparative Market Analysis

This is what real estate agents live by. It's a scientific approach to determining the value of your home by analyzing recent sales. Unlike simply taking the sales price of nearby homes, however, it compares them closely to see how similar they are to yours. And it uses sales over the past six months to a year as a database.

Why use recent home sales for comparison? It's because that's the best basis we have for determining the market. Remember, the cardinal rule in real estate is that a realistic price has nothing to do with what you paid for your home, what you owe on it, what you've put into the property, or what you "feel" it should be worth. Price is only what the market will bear.

How do you get a CMA, or a Comparative Market Analysis? You can call up any real estate agent, tell them you're interested in listing your home for sale, and almost certainly they'll be out to give you a presentation that should include a CMA. They can usually spin it out of their computer from the local MLS (Multiple Listing Service) database in a matter of minutes.

Keep in mind that you're under no obligation to actually list your property. And don't feel bad about asking for the CMA without listing. Agents typically "farm" areas. That means they will concentrate on a particular area and spend time with owners in the hopes of getting listings down the road, perhaps years from now. A good agent will be happy to come by once a year for five years or more giving you a CMA hoping that at the end of that time, when you finally decide to sell, you'll list with him or her. (Of course, for all that service, you should!)

Become a Looker

Before actually getting a CMA, I suggest that you become a looker, a pretend buyer for a weekend. You can easily do this to quickly gain a better knowledge of the housing market in your area. Go around to open houses and see what's out there. It won't take you very long at all to begin sizing up the market.

Pick a Date

Of course, you won't want to be doing this every weekend. Therefore, I suggest you pick a convenient date. Say it's around your birthday, the date when you bought your home, or a convenient holiday.

Once a year you'll take a few hours to determine what your home is worth by scouting out other properties on your own as a pretend buyer. Then you'll call in an agent (or do it yourself) and get a CMA to confirm your estimates.

What you need is a list of homes that have recently sold, sales prices (and original listing prices), and detailed descriptions of the homes. When you compare the houses on this list with your home, you'll get an accurate idea of what yours is worth.

Analyze the Comps

Once you have a list of comparables, you must do two things. First, you must analyze the list itself. That means you must make a judgment call about which homes that have been recently sold are actually similar to yours and which are not. You can even drive by several of the most apparently comparable homes to confirm your choices.

When you get the list of comparables, first check that they have the same number of basic features: square footage, bedrooms, baths, and exposure on the street (corner lot, inside lot, flag lot, etc.). Next check the amenities. If your home has a pool, do the comps? What about air conditioning? A spa? Larger lot? And so on.

Immediately eliminate those houses that are obviously dissimilar. Also, watch out for the oddball. If there is one sale on the list that seems suspiciously low compared with the others and another suspiciously high, throw them out. Chances are there was something unusual about the sale that you might never know about. (The seller was divorcing and had to take the first offer no matter how low, or the buyer fell in love with the property and paid far too much for it.)

TIP—DON'T LOOK WITH YOUR HEART

It's all too easy when looking at a list of comparables to automatically focus on the highest-priced home and then figure that's what your home is worth. Be realistic. Did that top-dollar home have lots of amenities that yours doesn't have?

Be Sure the Sales Are Current

The real estate market is constantly in a state of flux. Prices that are more than six months old might be out of date. Your house could be worth considerably more—or less.

Be wary of prices that are more than a year old. In the past, many markets moved glacially, and checking prices over a year old was an honest way to determine values. But in recent years with prices bouncing upward, it's a fool's method. You'll end up with an unrealistically low price for your home.

Be Sure to Check Only the Sales Price

These lists typically give both sales and a listing price. Normally, the listing price is much higher. (In some very hot markets, it's actually lower!)

Be sure you're looking at sales prices. You want to know what the homes actually sold for, not what prices the sellers initially hoped to get.

TRAP—SALES FIGURES ARE DELAYED

Keep in mind that normally the sales price for a home is not disclosed until after escrow closes. That's to protect a seller in case the deal falls through. If other buyers know what the seller actually was willing to sell for in the last deal, they will automatically come in with that price or lower in the next. Hence, agents normally won't disclose the actual sales price until the deal closes.

Check for Trends

Of course, with comps you're looking at past sales. However, the market is rarely static. Usually it's moving upward or downward. Now you can use some of those statistics that you might have been reading about in the paper.

For example, if you've noted that prices in your zip code are moving up at 10 percent a year and the comps you have are six months old, then adjust them upward by 5 percent. That should give you a more realistic sense of prices.

Similarly, to determine what your home will be worth in six months from now, adjust them another 5 percent upward. You could continue to project years in the future in this manner.

Of course, there's nothing to say that what happened in the past will be duplicated in the future. Just remember, it's an estimate, a guess. But if the current trend continues, it's likely to become reality. Just keep in mind that projections more than a year out into the future become really "iffy."

TIP—ESTIMATES CAN BECOME REALITY

If prices are trending upward, you could miss out on a big price hike if you decide to sell or refi because you were looking at prices that are six months or more old. Projections about future prices can help determine true value. Just remember that these projections might or might not come true. And they can project downward as well as up.

One way to help confirm trends is to ask an agent about inventory. This refers to the number of homes available for sale at any given time. Most agents will say that the current inventory is "high," "about average," or "low" depending on market conditions.

"High" means that there are more homes than normal for sale, and it will take a long time to sell them. This indicates a soft or weak market where prices might be expected to fall.

"Low" means there are few homes for sale, meaning that there's probably strong demand and they will move quickly. This usually portends a good market with prices moving up.

"About average" means a stagnant market where there are about as many buyers as sellers and prices should remain fairly constant.

You can also ask about how long it would take to sell the entire current inventory. This is given in months. Typically, anything under three months to sell the inventory indicates a hot market. Three to eight months is about average. More than eight months indicates a slow market.

Check Out the Houses

You've got a list of four (or however many) home sales that you believe are comparable to yours. But are they really? Maybe they're all painted purple, have terrible landscaping, or are on awkward-shaped lots on heavily trafficked streets. Maybe they're smaller or bigger, have more or fewer baths; maybe their condition and location within the neighborhood makes them much worse—or better!

Check out what the old listings (which is what the comp info is based on) actually say. (See Table 8.1.)

Table 8.1 Comparing Information

	House 1	House 2	House 3	House 4	Your House
Sq. ft.	_____	_____	_____	_____	_____
Bedrooms	_____	_____	_____	_____	_____
Bath	_____	_____	_____	_____	_____
Stories	_____	_____	_____	_____	_____
Lot size	_____	_____	_____	_____	_____
View	_____	_____	_____	_____	_____
Curb appeal	_____	_____	_____	_____	_____
Landscaping	_____	_____	_____	_____	_____
Traffic	_____	_____	_____	_____	_____
Condition	_____	_____	_____	_____	_____
Fireplace(s)	_____	_____	_____	_____	_____
Air	_____	_____	_____	_____	_____
Garages	_____	_____	_____	_____	_____
New windows	_____	_____	_____	_____	_____
Roof (tile, shingle, etc.)	_____	_____	_____	_____	_____
Pool	_____	_____	_____	_____	_____
Spa	_____	_____	_____	_____	_____
Other amenities	_____	_____	_____	_____	_____

Making the Comparison

It's rare that the comp houses will be identical to yours, although in a tract of homes this can happen. Your goal is to identify similarities and differences.

Once you've done this, it's time to do the math. The quickest, though not necessarily the best, way to do this is to simply add up the prices for all the comp homes and divide by the number, thus giving you an average value, which you can figure is probably the price you could get for your home.

It's going to be close, but to get a more accurate figure, I suggest you instead go through the following procedure. It won't take long.

Look for the Oddball

Sometimes there's one house that will throw your skew off. Someone might have overbuilt for the neighborhood and added a thousand more square feet than any surrounding house. It sold for $100,000 more than nearly any other house, too.

Or perhaps there's one house that's completely run-down. The owners have let it go to pot. It needs paint, the landscaping is minimal, and the garage door is hanging at a bad angle.

Don't figure this house in the mix. Take it out. Yes, the oddball will indeed influence neighborhood values upward or downward, but this should already be reflected in the prices of your other comp houses. Simply eliminating the oddball will keep your values from being skewed upward or downward.

Analyze the Similar Comps

As I said, it's unlikely any comp is going to be exactly like your house. Therefore, the easiest way to figure in the differences between yours is to use the plus (+) and minus (−) system. For each feature that a comp has that's better than yours, give it a plus. For each feature that isn't as nice as your house, give it a minus.

TIP—ASSIGN AN AMOUNT TO DIFFER- ENCES

This can be very difficult. After all, if another house has an extra bedroom, how much more is it worth than yours, or contrarily, how much less is yours worth? A detailed analysis will assign dollar amounts to differences.

Assuming you're just going to use the plus and minus system, go through all the comps and very quickly you'll have a list of plusses and minuses. Some comps might have three minuses, others five plusses. (Note: if a comp has a particularly nice feature better than your house, you might want to give it more than one plus. Do the same with minuses.)

Rating Comps Example

House 1	House 2	House 3	House 4	Your House
−++	−+	++	++++++	???

Now check out the range of the comps. Typically the homes sold will be in a fairly tight range. For example, you might have four houses, and their range of sales prices might be something like this:

Sales Price Range Example

House 1	House 2	House 3	House 4	Your House
$225,000	$215,000	$230,000	$240,000	???

When you compare the sales prices with how you've earlier rated the comps, a pattern will typically emerge. The homes that sold for more usually had features better than yours. The ones that had lower prices typically had features worse than yours.

In the listings we have noted that the highest-priced home, the one that sold for $240,000, we also gave five plusses to for better features. The one that sold for the lowest price, $215,000, we have the most minuses to.

Price Ranges

It's important to understand that in any given neighborhood, there will be a range of prices. Some homes will sell for more, others for less. Indeed, your own home might sell within a range of prices. Your goal, of course, is to determine what that range is.

Extrapolating from our above list, we would probably judge that the price range for the subject home is going to between $220,000 and $230,000. The house that sold for more, $240,000, we've already rated as having many more features (plusses) than our home and so is pretty much out of the range.

Those homes that had similar features to ours sold within the $10,000 range. If we had assigned values to the features instead of just plusses and minuses, we might now be able to derive a more accurate price range, perhaps down to an actual price for our home. Using just plusses and minuses, however, it's probably fair to say that our home's value is roughly $225,000.

Don't Forget to Add in Trends

Remember, we discussed the fact that the market is always moving. If the comps were six months old and prices are moving up 10 percent a year, we would want to add about 5 percent to the value we have, or $11,250 to the value of our home, boosting its current value to $236,250.

It's important to remember to allow for trends. This is a big mistake that many sellers make during periods of rapid price appreciation. They price their houses at what they were worth three or six months earlier, not what trends make them worth today. That's a quick way to lose money.

The Bottom Line on Price

Okay, if you're going to sell today, that's what you might hope to get for your property. Of course, people generally pay slightly less than asking price, so you might want to bump it up a bit. Ask an agent how much lower than asking price homes are going for. It might be 5 percent, 10 percent, zero percent, or in some hot markets, they might be selling for more than list.

On the other hand, buyers are very price conscious. Price it too high and most buyers won't even consider making an offer on it. They'll think of you as an unrealistic buyer.

Don't Forget
Transaction Costs

We're doing this mainly as an exercise to see what your home will net out to you, what its value to you really is. In order to do this, however, we also have to subtract the costs of sale.

TRAP—MARKET
VALUE

 Remember, what you paid for it, what you owe on it, how much you spent on it doesn't really count. It's only what the market says that it's worth that counts.

Earlier we said that transaction costs can easily be 8 to 10 percent of your home's value. You'll certainly want to figure this into any calculations of pricing that you make.

However, it's important to keep in mind that your actual costs might be more—or less. Also keep in mind that many of the seller's transaction costs, notably the commission, are different from the costs you paid when you purchased. Let's look at them more closely.

Commission

The most widely quoted commission rate is 6 percent. However, the rate is not fixed or standardized. It is whatever seller and agent agree upon. Studies have shown that the rate most commonly paid in recent years is closer to 5 percent. And there are many discount brokers who regularly charge less than that.

Of course, you tend to get what you pay for. If you want a full-service broker who handles all of the details of the transaction for you, from putting up the sign in front, to finding the buyer, to handling the closing, you'll probably end up paying top dollar.

On the other hand, if you're willing to do some of the work yourself, such as paying for advertising, showing the property, fielding phone calls, and so on, you can expect to pay less. And if you opt to sell FSBO or "By Owner," theoretically there might be no commission at all to pay.

TRAP—BE READY TO PAY A BUYER'S AGENT'S COMMISSION

Even if you sell on your own "by owner," you can expect that most buyers will be working with an agent. They will want to use that agent to protect their interests in the deal, and they will expect you to pay that agent's fee. (Either buyer or seller can pay the agent, but it's been so engrained that sellers usually pay that buyers simply expect it.) A buyer's agent's fee is typically half the normal fee, usually between 2.5 and 3 percent. It usually will be your cost.

Thus, realistically speaking, you can expect your real estate commission on selling to range from a low of about 2-½ percent to a high of about 5 to 6 percent. To determine if you're going to be on the high or low end, ask yourself if you're willing to put in the time and effort to sell your own home.

If you realistically answer no, than go for the high end. If you're the sort who looks forward to doing things on your own, look to the low end.

Title Insurance and Escrow

These can be paid by either buyer or seller or split. It usually hinges on local custom, although with the high fees charged these days, splitting is quickly becoming the most common.

The fee will vary according to the price of the home that's sold, market conditions, and which title insurance/escrow company you use. An old rule of thumb is that these fees were around 1 to 2 percent of the sales price.

Fix-up Costs

In order to sell your property, you will undoubtedly have to get a termite clearance (or else almost no lender will offer buyer's financing). Do you have termites in your house? Most people don't know. How much will it cost to remove them and fix any damage they've done? (Usually a seller's cost.) It's hard to say until you actually have the home inspected and the exterminator gives you a price.

Also, buyers will almost certainly insist on their own professional inspection of the property, and this could turn up all sort of unpleasantness. It's not uncommon for a buyer to demand a new roof, or at least an expensive fix of an old roof. Or a new heating/air conditioning system. Or fixing a foundation, or whatever.

The costs of fixing up your home for sale are the big unknowns. They could be tens of thousands of dollars. Or they could be almost nothing.

You could, of course, get a termite inspection and a professional inspection report yourself on an annual basis. However, that would cost you money (probably around $500 to $600 for both) and unless you're planning to sell soon, could be wasted money because they usually expire within a few months and new reports would be needed when you actually sell.

TIP—IF YOU SUSPECT
A PROBLEM

If you suspect a termite, structural, or other problem in your home, getting an inspection now long before you intend selling might be in order. It could expose the problem, thus allowing you to remedy it before it gets worse. Further, if the problem involves health and safety, finding and fixing it could ensure that you're living in a safer home. And, finally, knowing about it early on gives you lots of time to find the least expensive method of curing it.

As noted, it's not really possible to tell what problems you might have with fixing up the property until you're ready to sell. However, you might just throw in a figure to allow for it, knowing that it could be wildly off. I usually figure 2 percent.

Thus you can add up your transaction costs. We're going to assume here that you hire an agent to sell your home at a 5-percent commission, that title insurance and escrow are 1 percent of the sales price, and that there's 2 percent in fix-up and other closing costs. (See Table 8.2.)

If your examination of comparables tells you that your home is worth $300,000, then in our example, your net, after paying trans-

Table 8.2 Transaction Costs to Sell a $300,000 Home

Commission	5%	$15,000
Title Ins. and escrow	1%	3,000
Fix-up and other costs	2%	6,000
Totals	8%	$24,000

action costs would $276,000. That's what you could likely get out of your home if you were interested in selling it today. Of course, you're not, are you?

TRAP—OTHER TRANSACTION COSTS

Keep in mind that there will be other costs such as prorations. These are calculated between a buyer and seller who owes such things as taxes, insurance, and interest based on a certain date (typically close of escrow), loan payoff fees, title clearing, and so on. These could add to your costs at the time you sell.

Knowing Your Net

Knowing the net value of your home can be comforting, or disturbing, depending on how agreeable you find the figures. However, knowing is almost always better than not knowing—or guessing wrong.

TIP—KNOW YOUR EQUITY

Remember that the net worth of your home is not usually what you have in it. Your interest in it is your equity, the difference between what your home is worth and what you owe. In our example if the home is worth $276,000 after costs and you owe $200,000 on a mortgage, your equity is $76,000. That's the size of the check you'll get when you sell.

Your Equity	
Net Value of home	$276,000
Less Mortgage (s)	<u>200,000</u>
Equity	76,000

Chart Your Home's Value

As I suggested, it can be useful to go through this exercise at least once a year. (It goes very quickly, once you get the hang of it.) That way you can chart your home's value. (Some programs such as MS Money and Quicken allow you to create actual charts to show this.)

By referring to this chart, at any given time you can get a fairly accurate idea of what your home is worth, how much you owe (from your lender's mortgage statements) and your equity. Thus, if you need to quickly refi or sell, you won't be in the dark. (See Table 8.3.)

Should I Get an Appraiser?

You've done your homework and you have an excellent idea of what your house is worth. But you're still not sure. Should you call in a professional? Not unless you have money to blow.

You can get a professional appraiser to give you a qualified *opinion* as to the value of your house. The cost is usually around $300 to

Table 8.3 Home Valuation Chart

	Net Value	Mortgage	Equity
2004	$276,000	$200,000	$76,000
2005	?	?	?
2006			
2007			
2008			
2009			
2010			

$500. Real estate agents and mortgage brokers can recommend appraisers. Also, you can look for an appraiser in the phone book and the Internet under that heading.

Find an appraiser who has either an MAI or SREA designation. A registered appraiser should give you a written opinion of value. It will undoubtedly take into account comparables. Of course, the bottom line is that the appraisal will give you, presumably, one figure—the value of your home. You can see how it compares with the figure you arrived at by checking comparables on your own.

My own advice is to just do the work we've outlined above in this chapter. It can be fun to do, and going through the steps will help convince you of its accuracy. Besides, unless you're going to actually sell your house soon, why bother spending money on a professional appraiser.

What about an Agent's Appraisal?

You can also get an agent to give you an opinion as to the value of your home. Most agents will do this for free in the hopes of getting a listing out of you. (Of course you need not list just to get an appraisal.)

**TRAP—DON'T PAY
FOR AN AGENT'S
APPRAISAL**

Make sure an agent gives you a *written* appraisal and that it is understood up front that there will be no charge. A very few agents might offer appraisals, then send the owner a bill for several hundred dollars for the "work." These agents are not in the business of selling real estate, but in the business of making appraisals. Beware of them. Be sure you have it in writing that either the appraisal is free or that, if there is a charge, you know up front what it is and that you agree to it.

You might be asking yourself why you should bother with going through all the evaluation process if an agent can give you an appraisal in just a few minutes. My answer is confidence. Your own appraisal has one big advantage. You can totally trust yourself. You know the work you did and the effort you put forth.

Yes, it's nice to see if an appraiser or an agent agrees with you. (If they don't, you might want to check to see that you—or they—didn't make some gross error.) But if you do it yourself, you know how the price was calculated. You're not worried that someone is trying to pull the wool over your eyes.

And later on when it's time to sell, you'll know what your home is really worth. Any time an agent or buyer tries to knock the price down, you'll have the confidence to hold to your guns and stick to your price.

Part 2

A Home Operating Manual

9

The *Before* You Move in Checklist

You've bought your new home (at least it's new to you) and escrow has just closed. Your agent or the seller presents you with the official symbol of ownership, the keys to your new house. The movers are on the way and you're ready to move in.

Stop!

Before you move anything into your new house, take about half an hour to go through and carefully assess what you've bought. Look at the home from three perspectives:

- Health and safety
- Cleanup and repair
- Improvements

The time to do this is *before* you move in, when the home is vacant and empty. You'll never get another chance like this once you begin lugging in your furniture.

TRAP——BUT WHAT IF I HAD A HOME INSPECTION?

 Having a professional home inspection, particularly by a member of a national association such as ASHI (American Society of Home Inspectors—www.ashi.com) or NAHI (National Association of Home Inspectors— www.hahi.org) is certainly a good thing. Trained inspectors can uncover a lot of problems that the home might have. But chances are that your home inspection was weeks if not months ago. Things might have changed since then. Further, when the home inspection took place, chances are the seller's furnishings were in the home, there were carpets on the floors, and clothing in closets. Inspectors normally do not look anywhere that's not accessible. Now, presumably, the home is empty and you can see so much more.

Wouldn't I be better off to have another home inspection?

It certainly couldn't hurt. But that will cost you another $350 or so. Further, chances are that you might be able to spot many of the troubles that are likely to occur in an inspection of your own. And, if you do the inspection, you'll remember what you saw so that at the end of the year when you do your annual maintenance inspection (see Chapter 12), you'll be able to more easily note any changes or problems.

The following is not intended to substitute for a professional home inspection. However, it should help alert a new home owner to problems that might be present in the home.

Health and Safety Check

1. **Use your nose**.

    Walk through the home and check for odors. The home should smell fresh and clean, even with the doors and windows closed. Some odors to watch out for are:

    ☐ **Rotten egg or sulfur smell**—Might indicate leaking gas. This could result in an explosion. Immediately vacate the home and call the gas company or the fire department. Sometimes when people move out, a line to a gas dryer might be damaged or left slightly open and gas could be accumulating in the house. The usual remedy is to open all doors and windows to evacuate the gas and have a plumber identify and fix the line.

    ☐ **Moldy or musty odor**—Might indicate mold growing. Most likely spots are anywhere there is water: in bathrooms, kitchens, and utility rooms. Also might occur under wall-to-wall carpets in homes with a concrete slab. Contact a pest removal company.

☐ **Sour garbage smell**——Might indicate rotting food or dead animal. Check the house thoroughly, particularly in kitchen and bathroom cabinets and in the garage might indicate plugged sewer line vents.

2. Look around.

Often you can spot problems simply by being aware of your surroundings. You should have already checked out the home during a "final walkthrough." However, now with the home cleaned out, things might seem different. Now you're looking to see if something has changed, something is off. Some things to pay special attention to are:

☐ **Windows, doors and screens**—Are any broken or missing? If so, you'll immediately want to tell your agent and the seller.

☐ **Holes and scratches in walls and ceilings, spots in carpet**—Expect these to appear when furniture is moved away. But if they are serious and new, you'll want to complain.

☐ **Evidence of rodent or pest**—These can break in when a house is unattended and make a nest. You'll probably want them evicted by a pest control company before you move in.

3. Check things out.

You'll want to make sure that everything is working okay. This includes lights and appliances, faucets and drains, and home systems such as heating and air. A word of caution, however, *Do not attempt any repairs to anything electrical unless the power is completely turned off. Do not attempt any repairs to anything gas. Call the gas company or a plumber.*

☐ **Water faucets and drains**—Flush each toilet several times to make sure it's draining. Also run the shower, tub, and sink to make sure the water goes down. If it collects or does not drain, a plumber might be in order.

☐ **Appliances**—Run each one through a cycle to make sure it works. If not, you might need to rely on your Home Warranty Plan (if you got one) or the agent/seller to get it fixed.

**TRAP—BE WARY
IF ANYTHING HAS
BEEN REPAIRED
OR REWIRED**

I recently moved into a home where there had been some remodeling. An electrician had done the electrical work, but had somehow crossed the wires in the 220-volt electric dryer plug. When it was plugged in the ground line and one of the current lines were switched, my wife received a strong shock from the dryer. I discovered that the metal surface of the dryer was giving off 110 volts! She could have been electrocuted. Be extremely wary if any appliance or plug has recently been repaired, rewired, or installed.

☐ **Lights and plugs**—You might need to supply light bulbs and fixtures, but they should all work.

☐ **Heater and air conditioner**—Turn these on and operate them for a time, even if the outside temperature is at an extreme. The furnace might need a new filter, and that's something many homeowners can handle. If you smell any gas exhaust in the house, it might indicate a problem. Shut off the heater/air conditioner and have a professional check it out.

☐ **Garage door to house**—This should be solid core door (for fire safety) and should swing closed automatically to be sure that exhaust gases from cars and elsewhere do not get into the home.

☐ **Garage door opener**—It should be set to allow it to stop and reverse should it hit anything or anyone. Modern garage door openers come equipped with this safety feature.

☐ **Water heater safety**—The water heater should have a temperature/pressure safety valve. Test it to be sure it's operative. (Note: sometimes with old heaters, checking the valve will cause it to malfunction in the open position.)

☐ **Elevated appliances in the garage**—Any gas appliance should be elevated at least 18 inches off the floor. This is to prevent an explosion and/or fire should gas fumes from your car or elsewhere accumulate.

☐ **Tie downs**—In earthquake and hurricane country, your water heater and other movable heaters/appliances should be tied down to avoid shaking and movement that could break them loose and possibly cause a fire in the event of a natural disaster. Check with your county for the approved method of tying them down.

☐ **Smoke detectors**—There should be one in every bedroom and every hallway as well as in major rooms. Check each one to be sure it's operative. If not, replace it and/or its batteries. Also, consider getting a carbon monoxide detector.

☐ **Fire extinguishers**—There should be one in the kitchen and garage and any other room where a fire might occur. If there aren't any, consider getting them.

☐ **Fences**—Walk the perimeter of the lot and make sure the fences are in order. This is particularly important if you have a pool or spa, as there is a liability issue. Gates should close automatically.

☐ **Fireplace**—Make sure it draws and works properly. A bad fireplace can cause a fire or release carbon monoxide into the house.

☐ **Door locks**—Immediately replace or rekey all the locks to the home. If you don't, the seller or a person to whom he lent a key, such as a workperson, might be able to gain access.

☐ **Roof, foundation, structure**—This was undoubtedly covered in your professional home inspection. But, you might want to check it out again for yourself. Beware of climbing in the attic of your house. You could fall, step through a roof, or otherwise hurt yourself. Beware of climbing under your home in the crawlspace. There could be bugs and you could hurt yourself. Don't walk on your roof—it's a long way down if you fall.

☐ **Check the other features of your home**—Make sure everything works before you move in.

☐ **Emergency numbers**—Be sure you know them for the police and fire departments as well as for the doctor and local hospital. Have them posted at a central location near the phone. Most people prefer the kitchen.

Cleanup and Repair Check

1. Condition of the paint

    Check the walls in every room. Also check the ceilings, but they aren't as important. Don't forget to look at the closets. If anything needs painting, now is the time to do it, before you move in. You might, in fact, want to delay your move in a day or two to allow time for painting. Or, alternatively, move the furniture from one room to another to allow for painting.

    ☐ Kitchen needs paint
    ☐ Master bedroom needs paint
    ☐ Bedroom needs paint
    ☐ Master bath needs paint
    ☐ Bathroom needs paint
    ☐ Living room needs paint
    ☐ Dining room needs paint
    ☐ Den needs paint
    ☐ Utility room needs paint
    ☐ _____ needs paint
    ☐ _____ needs paint

2. Condition of the carpeting

    You might want to vacuum the carpeting at the least, replace it at the most, and at least clean it in between. Remember, the carpeting was used by the previous owners and their germs, mold, and bugs are living in it.

TIP—CHECK CARPET-ING FOR PET ODOR

It's almost impossible to remove pet urine, especially from cats, from carpeting. The only sure method involves replacing the carpeting, padding, and at least cleaning the floor underneath. If there is a strong odor of pet urine in the carpeting, you might want to call your agent and the seller about a remedy such as getting all new carpeting from the seller. This is one of the things that can ultimately require the services of an attorney and court to resolve.

☐ Vacuum carpeting
☐ Have carpeting cleaned
☐ Replace carpeting

3. Window and screen cleaning
   It's rare that seller will leave a property and clean the windows and screens. It's something that new owners need to do. If you're going to do it, it's often easiest before you actually move in.

4. Garage cleaning
   Hopefully the previous owners got rid of all the garbage that accumulates in the garage. If not, it's your task.

Improvements

There are all sorts of home improvements that you might want to do over the first six months of ownership. However, when you first get possession of the house is often the best time to make an assessment of what should be done.

The reason is that you're getting a fresh look at the house without the clutter of furniture. You'll see things that over a period of months you'll get used to and forget about. You'll notice areas that are awkward that, after living in the home for awhile, will become familiar.

In other words, while now might not be the time to make improvements (undoubtedly you want to get on with moving in), now is an excellent time to note for the future what you want done.

1. Major improvements to consider for the future
   Add more space to:
   ☐ Living/dining room
   ☐ Master bedroom
   ☐ Additional bedroom
   ☐ Closet(s) in _____

2. Do a major/minor remodel to:
   ☐ Kitchen   Major ☐ Minor ☐
   ☐ Master bath   Major ☐ Minor ☐
   ☐ Bathroom   Major ☐ Minor ☐
   ☐ Master Bedroom   Major ☐ Minor ☐
   ☐ Other area _____

3. Redo landscaping in:
   ☐ Front
   ☐ Back
   ☐ Side   Left ☐ Right ☐

10

Surviving the Move

Moving, for most of us, is usually a rather unpleasant task. There are 101 different things we must remember to do from turning on the utilities to watering the violets. However, it's also a good time, or can be, because we're moving into our new home, and the world seems full of possibilities.

If this is your first move—or your second or even third to a new home, it's going to be helpful to have a list of things you should do to make the transition to your new home easier and more rewarding. That's what we'll attempt to accomplish in this chapter.

Arrange for the Hookup

This is one of the trickiest parts of moving into a new home. You're going to need phone service and utilities, not to mention newspaper and other deliveries.

But you might not exactly know what day escrow is going to close. So how do you give the various companies a day to start service?

My little trick is to tell a white lie. I pick the earliest possible day that I could move into the property. For example, escrow is scheduled to close on June 30th. But if something goes wrong, as it usually does, it will probably close later. Yes, it could close on time. But who can say? So I call all the service companies I need as early possible, hopefully in early May, and tell them I'm moving in on June 30th and want to be connected no later than that date.

TRAP—DO IT EARLY

In some communities, particularly where there's a lot of new building, it can take as long as six weeks for phone and utility hookups.

I get them all to agree to that early date, and then I wait. As it gets closer to the deadline, I might learn that things aren't going too well with my mortgage. It's going to take a little longer to clear up some errors that the credit reporting bureau made, or there's a problem with a loan payoff from years ago, or whatever. It looks like the deal won't actually close until July 10th.

So, when it gets close to June 30th and it's apparent the deal isn't going to close on time, I call the utilities and ask them for a slight postponement. They are usually happy to comply, although some companies might charge a fee for rescheduling.

The thing I've discovered is that these companies usually find it far easier to postpone establishing service once you have a firm date, than they do giving you that original date. I've repeatedly postponed without a problem until, perhaps just before the correct date, I've called and gotten the services installed right on time.

Of course, this doesn't mean that it will necessarily work for you. Your service company might say that if you don't meet the agreed-upon date, you'll need to go back to the beginning of the line. Or they might be happy to push installation back a day or two—or more.

Getting everything hooked up just when you want it during a move is one of the great games that new owners play. Here's a list of services you'll probably want to contact:

Services to Contact Weeks before You Move

- Phone (DSL)
- Cable TV (cable modem)
- Satellite
- Garbage pickup
- Water
- Natural gas (propane)

- Oil, coal, wood
- Electricity
- Newspaper(s)
- Pool/spa service
- Gardening service
- Other service

DSL or Cable Modem?

In addition to simply getting the service hooked up, you might be fortunate enough to have a choice between types of service. For example, if you want broadband Internet connection, you might have a choice of a cable modem or a DSL line. (Most of us get one or the other, but not both.)

If you have a choice, which should you opt for? You have to consider the speed of the service, connection charges, monthly costs, and any difficulty in getting it set up in the house just where you want it.

In my case, I have both DSL and a cable modem, each in a different location. And my experience has been that the prices are fairly comparable, the installation about as difficult (or easy) with either, and the speed roughly equivalent. The difference for me has been in the service.

I've found the cable modem service to be impeccable, once I got around some hardware problems. The DSL service, on the other hand, I've found to be spotty. Of course, a lot depends on which provider you're using and the equipment they have. Sometimes the modem itself can be the heart of the problem; other times it's simply a lot of downtime on the service.

Wired or Wireless?

It's possible to have many of your appliances, including cable or DSL lines, TV, and audio either wired or wireless within your home. Indeed, many modern homes now come wired for phone, TV, A/V, and computers. If yours is already wired, then by all means use what you have.

However, you should be aware that there are an increasing number of low-cost wireless options. For example, rather than stringing Cat-5 wire through your house (assuming it's not already in) for your computer, for a cost of less than $100, you can get a wireless hookup.

I've found NetGear to be a good manufacturer here. Simply connect a wireless router to your DSL or cable modem and a wireless receiver or nic (network interface connection) into the USB port of your computer. Add a dash of software drivers, and you should be up and running with no problems.

Wireless connections for your home entertainment system are also available from companies such as Sony and others. However, as of this writing, they rely primarily on infrared, hence they are line of sight. Out of sight (or if someone moves between sender and receiver) and the sound is gone. If your house isn't already wired, when you move in you might want to see if it's possible to go wireless and save yourself a huge wiring expense.

Getting the Move
Out of the Way

Once you've arranged for the utilities, or perhaps even before (weeks, perhaps months before you move), you should make arrangements for who will transport your furniture. This goes without saying. However, it's the sort of thing that most of us simply put off until the last minute.

There are a host of moving companies listed in the Yellow pages and on the Internet, and it's beyond the scope of this book to go into detail on how you should organize your move. However, a few tips from someone who has moved many times might prove helpful.

Get Started Early

As noted, the sooner you get to it the better. This gives you time to talk to several moving companies and compare prices and services.

Expect Problems

The movers don't show up on time, or their truck is too small to carry all your things, or they won't carry stuff down a stairway, or... It happens. Just accept it and work it out as best you can. Extra money usually helps grease the works and makes things run smoother.

There's More Than You Think

Whenever I move I'm astonished at how much I have to transport. The best advice is to throw away everything you absolutely don't need. This saves paying to have it moved to your new home and then having to throw it away.

Estimates Are Just That

I've found most movers to be honest people. However, reports in the press suggest that there are a lot of problems with moving, particularly when moving interstate. Try to get estimates from the major moving companies. Remember, in the final analysis, moving is usually by weight, and whomever you get is likely to charge a similar price. Further, estimates are based on what an estimator thinks your furniture is going to weigh. They can and are often wrong, at least a little bit. That means it might cost more (somehow it seldom costs less) than the estimate.

Breakage Happens

If you get insurance, be sure it's from a separate insuring company. If the company that moved you is self-insuring, it could delay filing claims and making payments.

It Might Not Arrive on Time

This could be your biggest concern. Your furniture and other things might be delayed and might not arrive when you want them to. Or worse yet, the movers suddenly show up a day before you get possession of the house and don't want to wait around, telling you they'll make another delivery and get back to you when they can. It's best to allow a window of several days, if possible, for the movers.

Get the Important Things Going Early

If you have children, they're going to need to attend school. If you drive to work, you're going to need to know the best routes. If you take mass transit, you'll need to know when the trains or buses run, and how to get to the stations. When you're going to go shopping, it's helpful to know where the nearest supermarket is.

Of course, you can do all of these things after you move in. However, if you have time, it's usually better to do them beforehand. That way, as soon as you get into the house you're ready to go. You can hit it running.

It's also a good idea to locate the nearest hospital with an emergency room, just in case. And get recommendations about physicians.

Drive by the house for a few days and see the easiest ways to get to shopping, work, and school. Of course, register your children in their schools early in case there's a lot of paperwork and transferring of files.

Finally, check out the local cultural events such as plays, musical events, even movie theaters. You don't want to move in and suddenly find you don't know what's happening outside your walls. (I myself like to search out the local pizza parlor so that I can have pizzas ordered for us during the move.)

Allow Yourself Time

Don't try to do it all at once. Rome wasn't built in a day, and moving doesn't have to be accomplished in one breathless dash. Allow time to rest, wash up, and go out (to a movie or play), and relax. Then take it up again another day.

The worst thing you can do is to strain a muscle or worse because you're working too hard on your move. Even if you have to move in over a period of days, weeks, or months, what's the difference in the final analysis? Once you're in, you won't remember how long it took, unless something unfortunate happened as part of the move.

11

Upgrading Your Home

If your home is 10 years old or older, then you might want to seriously consider upgrading it. Perhaps you feel that you'd like to live in more modern surroundings. With the way home appliances and fixtures have improved in recent years, you might want the greater convenience and efficiency of something new.

On the other hand, homes newer than 10 years rarely need updating because, presumably, they are already up-to-date. Nevertheless, even some newer homes might have features that you find are obsolete. In that case, updating might still be in order.

Most people upgrade their homes within the first six months to two years of ownership. After that, most of us tend to settle in and might not want to spend the money for upgrades until we begin considering selling.

If you are thinking of updating your home, then the first thing you must decide is what do you want to attack first? Is it the windows or doors? What about the heater and air conditioning system? Or maybe it's those old-fashioned "popcorn" ceilings that you'd like to eliminate.

In this chapter we're going to consider the most popular areas for updating. And we'll keep a special eye on how much it's likely to cost, as well as how much it's likely to get you in return when you sell.

Remove "Popcorn" Ceilings

To my mind, nothing dates a home so much as "popcorn" ceilings. If you don't know what these are, it's simple. Back in the 1950s and 1960s, (and sometimes even later), builders would often blow in the home's ceilings. They used a kind of material that typically included cellulose and sometimes asbestos—a dangerous substance that might cause cancer and other diseases. The blown-in material would adhere to the plasterboard ceiling and have a very rough texture. To many who looked at it, it seemed to look like popcorn, hence the name.

These ceilings were reputed to have sound dampening effects. Builders would often explain that because the ceiling was no longer flat, sound waves wouldn't bounce off it in parallel lines, but instead would be diffused in all directions. This, they felt, would mute the sound. Personally, I've never noticed any sound dampening effects from this ceiling.

At the height of their popularity, virtually all new homes included these ceilings. Sometimes tiny pieces of shiny metal would be mixed in, giving the ceilings a sparkling appearance, particularly at night.

By the 1990s, however, styles changed and most people became turned off by popcorn ceilings. Today the trend is to install flat ceilings the same texture as walls.

TIP—POPCORN CEILINGS ARE MAKING A COMEBACK!

Interestingly, some avant-garde builders are once again introducing popcorn ceilings, sans asbestos, as a "new" retro look!

One of the concerns with older popcorn ceilings is the asbestos material they might contain. People worry that asbestos might drop from the ceiling and contaminate items beneath it.

This is probably an unnecessary concern. Most asbestos is not a danger unless it is disturbed, and if popcorn ceilings are not touched, they probably don't present much of a health hazard.

What Are Your Options?

There are really only three realistic options with popcorn ceilings. The first is to simply leave them alone. Learn to live with them and accept the fact that your home has a more traditional look.

On the other hand, if you're concerned about the asbestos in them possibly flaking down, or if you simply want to change the color, you can encapsulate them. This is typically done by spraying the ceilings with shellac or other material that forms a sealed surface on the popcorn. They are then spray painted to any color you might desire. It's probably not a good idea to shellac or paint a popcorn ceiling using a brush or rollers, as this could disturb the ceiling and possibly release asbestos into the atmosphere.

Finally, you can have the popcorn removed. This process usually begins by having a professional take a sample of the ceiling to determine if it, indeed, does contain asbestos. (Asbestos was generally no longer in use in ceilings by the 1980s, but your home could be an exception.) The only way to determine this is by a laboratory analysis. The cost is usually less than $400.

If your popcorn ceiling does not contain asbestos, then the usual method is to cover the entire floor and walls with plastic, spray the ceiling with water (which mixes readily with the popcorn material), and scrape it off. Once off, the ceiling typically must be taped, retextured, and repainted.

If your ceiling does contain asbestos, then the above process is also used. However, the entire house is typically "bubbled" and special filters are used to capture any asbestos that is introduced into the atmosphere. Only a professional asbestos mitigation company should be used to remove asbestos ceilings.

**TRAP—DO NOT
ATTEMPT TO
REMOVE ASBESTOS
YOURSELF**

Asbestos fibers are incredibly small and you might ingest them or release them into the environment where they could threaten others.

What Are the Typical Costs?

If your popcorn ceiling does not contain asbestos, whole house removal including taping, retexturing, and repainting typically starts at around $2500, depending on the size of the house. Remember, of course, that you also have to add in the cost of having the ceiling tested for asbestos.

On the other hand, if the ceiling does contain asbestos, the price could easily be $10,000 or more. It all depends on the layout and air circulation in your home. The only way to know is to get a reliable estimate from a professional asbestos mitigation company.

What Are You Likely to Recoup?

Once again, it's very hard to put a figure on this. A lot depends on how different the appearance of your house is before and after.

Many buyers today automatically subtract a figure for removing popcorn ceilings from any offer they make. The reason is that to some people, it's simply anathema. Popcorn ceilings, to them, speak of old-fashioned and out of style. Thus, by removing the popcorn ceilings, you could get a significantly higher bid from this type of buyer.

On the other hand, other people simply don't care. To them it's nothing whether there's "popcorn" on the ceiling or not. Indeed, they might even enjoy it!

Thus, the difficulty in determining how much, or even IF, you can recoup your dollars when you sell. If it only costs a few thousand to do this, then you might very well recoup every dime you spend. On the other hand, if you have asbestos and it costs tens of thousands to do the job, you might have difficulty in getting your money back.

My own suggestion is that you do this upgrade mainly to please yourself. If it makes living in the house better for you (or you worry about asbestos in your ceiling), don't worry about the recouping the cost. You'll more than make up for it in personal enjoyment.

Adding New Windows

Many older homes (more than 10 to 15 years old) came with single-pane and/or with metal frame windows. These windows certainly do the job when it comes to keeping the rain out. However, they leave a great deal to be desired when it comes to controlling heat, cold, and sunlight.

In areas of extreme temperatures, double-pane windows have been the rule for many years, in some cases even triple pane.

However, while these cut heat loss/gain in winter/summer in half, they pale in comparison to the job that modern double-pane windows do.

Typically, metal frame windows are set without wood molding around them into the window area and, if they contain steel, over time often show signs of rust. Both steel- and aluminum-frame windows can bind after a few years due to home settling.

Further, metal-frame windows tend to set the age of the home. If you haven't noticed it, I'm sure your visitors have. And if you try to sell your home, these old–style, metal-frame windows are sure to knock your price down and make the home harder to sell.

Your Options

Today you have many options when it comes to windows. The most popular are vinyl, although some of the finest windows are wood and metal combinations. (The wood virtually surrounds the metal, which is used for strength.)

Whatever window style you choose, you should seriously consider getting double pane, even in moderate climates. Further, you should look into low-e (emissivity). Low-e double-pane windows have an R-rating (which refers to their ability to resist heat transfer) of about R-5 to R-7. This compares to single-pane glass, which is about R-1 and double pane without low-e, which is about R-2. What this means is that the windows will let less heat in during the summer and transmit less house heat out during the winter.

You also have two basic choices: You can either replace the windows (take out the old ones and put in new ones) or retrofit them (explained below). The primary method of replacement is to simply remove the old windows and install new ones. This, however, means that whatever siding you have on the outside of your house will be disturbed. If you have stucco, it means that you'll need to do extensive patching. Wood can generally be removed and replaced more easily. Almost certainly the exterior walls in which you do the replacement will have to be repainted, which for a whole house means a complete repainting of the property.

Your other choice is to use retrofitted windows. These are made by Milgard and other companies. Instead of removing the existing window frames, they are carefully measured and retrofits are specifically made for each window. Then the windows themselves (not the frames) are removed and replaced. The entire process only takes about an hour for each window. You have your choice of using the old molding or having new molding installed.

About the only problems I've run into with vinyl windows is that when they are retrofitted, the larger ones (six feet and over) sometimes do not open and close easily. Thus you might be better off selecting a combination window (several small windows combined into one), rather than a very large single.

What Does It Cost?

A whole house window retrofit (using the old frames) typically costs around $8000 to $10,000 for an average-size home of 2000 square feet. It comes with vinyl casings for the windows. If you want more elaborate moldings, you'll have to contract with a carpenter to handle these for you. (They are well worth the usually slight additional cost because of their far superior appearance.)

If you want to completely replace the existing windows with new ones, the cost is more, mainly because of the repair work that will need to be done to the exterior of the home. Whether you replace or retrofit, chances are your new windows will have to be made to order. Standard windows typically found in building supply stores such as Lowes or Home Depot will not fit the exact sizes of windows put into homes decades ago. (You could, of course, get lucky! The cost of a standard-sized ready-made window is about half that of one made just to fit your particular needs.)

TRAP—YOU'LL NEED TO REPAINT

Don't forget painting costs. With retrofitting, you normally do not need to repaint, as there is little to no damage inside or out. With replacement, however, painting is almost a must. These days a whole-house exterior painting can run between $2000 and $3000 for an average 2000-square-foot home.

Of course, keep in mind that with new windows, your utility bills are likely to plummet. Many people report savings of 10 to 40 percent when new, more efficient windows are put in place in their homes.

What Are You Likely to Recoup?

This, of course, is the big question that everyone asks. How much more will I get when I eventually sell?

Unfortunately, the truth of the matter is that it is impossible to give a definitive answer. How much more you'll add to the value of your home with new windows differs with each home.

In homes where the old windows were unsightly and distracting, new windows should add significantly to the value of the home, perhaps as much as 70 percent of the cost of the windows. This amount will also be affected when switching to more efficient windows in areas of extreme climate.

Keep in mind that today's homebuyers are increasingly sophisticated. When they see that your home has modern, new windows, they are likely to pay more, and even more likely to make a bid on the property.

New Window Coverings

Whether your windows are new or old, you need to cover them with something. Window coverings help keep out sunlight that can bleach carpeting and furniture. They also are necessary if you are going to have privacy in your home. This is particularly the case with newer homes. which tend to be built close together.

Many people who buy resales (existing homes) keep the window coverings that come with the property. It's easier and certainly less expensive to live with what someone else put into the house. However, over time most of us prefer to replace those old window coverings with new ones more suited to our own tastes.

What Are Your Options?

The only limit to window coverings is really your imagination. In the old days, window coverings were typically drapes, curtains, and shades or some combination of all three.

Today, however, any and all sorts of things can and do serve as window coverings, including:

Common Window Coverings

- Drapes (with or without valances)
- Curtains
- Shades (conventional, pleated, semiopaque)
- Blinds
  - Plantation style
  - Venetian style of wood or vinyl
  - Vertical style of wood, plastic, or cloth
- Sheets of cloth
- Fiberglass sheeting (semitransparent)
- Screening (inside or outside)
- Opaquing glass (that can electronically turn opaque or transparent)
- Swinging doors

What Are the Typical Costs?

The costs of covering windows can sometimes be almost as high as the cost of putting in replacement windows! To have a whole house done in Venetian style vinyl window slats can easily cost $1200 to $2000. (You can pick up these windows at building supply stores such as Home Depot or Lowes for about $50 apiece, have them cut to your window's dimensions, and install them yourself. The installation is not difficult, but you will have to spend some time adjusting lengths. And the materials tend to be heavy.)

If you opt for plantation-style windows (they typically have a wood piece in the center that is used to open and close them), the costs will probably double. If you use special woods and have the windows stained (as opposed to simply having them painted), the costs could easily triple.

A newer trend in window coverings is the use of a variety of materials that are semitransparent. They let light in and allow you to see out somewhat. They shade severe light and in most situations keep people from looking in. These usually have to be custom fitted and can cost around $150 for a window (twice that for a slider door). These are also available as sun-shading screens. *Note: Be wary of installing sun-shading screen on the inside when you have double-pane windows. The screens could force heat back at the window and eventually cloud or otherwise damage the area between the panes.* Check with manufacturer.

The price of conventional drapes and curtains varies enormously according to the quality of the material and whether you have it installed professionally or do so yourself. At the low end, you can have a whole house done for around $1000. The sky's the limit at the upper end.

What Are You Likely to Recoup?

Unfortunately, though you might spend a fortune on window coverings, your chances are probably nil for recouping the money you spent in the form of a higher price for your home when you sell. Most people expect the home they buy to come with window coverings. If the coverings are elaborate and make the house look wonderful, so much for the better, most buyers will figure. But very few buyers will add to the price tag because you've spent extra money on window coverings.

If you're putting in window coverings with an eye to selling, my advice is to go with those that reflect what's common in your neighborhood. Do not spend a lot of money. Do not buy the most expensive. Get the lowest common denominator—buy window coverings that look nice but don't set you back a bundle in cash.

New Doors

This is a tricky subject. With the exception of exterior doors (which we'll come to in a moment) adding new doors to the inside of your home usually won't make your house any more energy efficient. Indeed, adding new interior doors usually won't make any difference, except for appearance. And there, they can make all the difference in the world.

Many older tract homes come with flat veneer interior doors. The veneer might be painted a color to match the walls, or it might be kept as a natural wood that's been stained. Almost always they are hollow core, which means that interior of the door is empty—it has a frame and veneer on both sides with a few pieces of cardboard in between for support. It's a hollow door. The molding around the door is also frequently only about an inch wide and is flat in appearance.

The problem with these interior doors, whether in wood or painted, is that they identify the house as tract-built and old-fashioned. Although there is nothing basically wrong with these doors, they are often too simple to allow your home to have an elegant air.

Exterior doors, particularly on the front, are more important, as they set the tone for the quality of the home. In many older homes, the front doors are simply a variety of the same door that was used inside, except that for security and fire safety, it's almost always solid core—filled with wood or sometimes a cementlike material.

The front doors are portals to your home. If the portals have a rich look, then most visitors' first impressions are that your home is richly outfitted. If they are plain looking, well, you can guess what the impression is going to be. It's for this reason that many home-owner's first upgrade in a home is to install new front doors.

Sliders are doors that typically lead to patios or garden areas to the side or rear of the home. The problem with these is that over the years, if they are wood, they might have rotted out due to regular exposure to moisture. If they are metal, they might bind and become difficult to move. Additionally, metal sliders often look old and tired.

What Are Your Options?

Most newer homes come with paneled doors that, though still composed of veneers and hollow cores, strike us a having a kind of classic beauty and modernity. These newer doors have a variety of panels extruded from the surface on both sides. They typically come in two-, four-, and six-panel varieties. And the surface can either be flat or simulated wood-grain. These doors are usually made of fiberglass.

When it comes to front doors, there's almost no limit to the varieties available. You can, of course, use a door similar to those described for the inside—upraised panels with or without wood grain. Other varieties (all solid core) include:

- Solid wood doors (mahogany, oak, spruce, ash, and many other woods)—these are usually stained to show off the wood grain

- Glass-paneled solid wood door inserts (the glass panels can be plain, etched, opaque, stained, or otherwise treated)

- Fiberglass, wood veneer, or metal doors, usually with panels, sometimes with glass panels

- Double doors or doors with a side panel next to the door.

- Exotic doors with intricate patterns carved onto the surface often reflecting South Seas or African themes

Further, there's all sorts of hardware that's available for front doors. You can choose from the simplest to the most ornate. Also check into Chapter 7 on security issues for front door hardware.

Sliders are commonly made of vinyl frames. Be sure they use safety glass. The same conditions apply to them as to the new vinyl windows noted above.

TRAP—SLIDERS CAN BE HEAVY

 Be aware, however, that vinyl sliders more than 6 feet wide can be very difficult to open and close.

Of course, you could opt for a variety of paneled sliders, which either are authentic (true panels of glass) or have a panel weave inserted between two panes of double-pane glass to give illusion of panels.

What Are the Typical Costs?

New interior doors are amazingly inexpensive. At building supply stores you can commonly find them as prehung (they're set in their frame) for as little as $30 to $50 apiece. This includes a variety of paneled and wood grain doors. Ordered individually from custom manufacturers they run about twice that in price.

Of course, keep in mind that when installing new interior doors, you'll have to remove the existing molding and replace it with new decorative molding. This can get expensive, but it will usually yield you a much finer looking doorway.

Replacing all the interior doors within a house, including putting on new molding and having it professionally done will typically cost between $1500 and $2000 for a standard 2000-square-foot house. Of course, the price can zoom up if you select expensive molding and fancier doors.

New front doors, although they also come prehung, must usually be professionally installed. The reason is that they must fit right within the frame to be weathertight, and they must be adequately attached to provide security for the home.

Often owners will opt for oak or another wood finish, many times with ornate glass embellishment. Complete the package with a polished gold, silver, or the new platinum look in hardware, and the entrance to your home can look truly elegant.

The doors themselves can cost anywhere from a minimal door of around $300, to a solid hardwood door costing $3000 to a more ornate set of double doors costing $6000 and up. Hardware for the door is typically an additional $100 or so, and expect to pay several hundred dollars to have a professional hang it.

Putting in new sliders depends on whether you use replacements or retrofits (see windows, above). Replacements run about $250 to $500 for a 6-foot or 8-foot door. Retrofits are roughly twice that price. Note that many professionals refuse to retrofit sliders, arguing that the retrofit process does not allow them to be sufficiently well attached.

What Are You Likely to Recoup?

While it's hard to say, my own feeling is that if by adding new doors you change the feel of the home from one of an inexpensive tract house to that of a custom home, it can add thousands of dollars to the price, sometimes as much as the cost of all the doors.

Replacing all of your home's doors, exterior and interior, can literally revolutionize your property's appearance. Suddenly buyers can see value where they couldn't see it before.

If you're thinking of selling in the future and your home has old-fashioned doors, seriously consider upgrading them. It could make a big difference to buyers. (Of course, it could also make an enormous difference to your enjoyment of the home while you live there.)

Room Heaters

These have become popular in recent years in response to the high cost of heating a home in the winter. Additionally, they offer a kind of beauty that's taken from Victorian-era homes.

Today, particularly, in areas where the weather is colder, the cost of heating an entire home has sometimes doubled or more. It really doesn't matter whether you use natural gas, propane, electric, oil, coal, or even wood. Whole house heating costs have skyrocketed. (In areas where coal and wood are used, concerns about pollution have led to limiting their use, or requiring that expensive high-efficiency stoves be used.)

As a result, one alternative increasingly considered is heating only one room, or a small group of rooms. Instead of firing up a central heater to handle the whole house, a separate heater is installed in one area of the house. It produces heat and warms only that area.

Of course, this won't work if you use all of your house. But most of us don't use our entire house. Perhaps we use one or two bedrooms and a living area and kitchen. Indeed, in some cases half or two-thirds of typical homes can be closed off and kept at a minimum temperature. For example, your whole house heater can be set to keep all of the rooms in the home at a cool 60 degrees. However, those rooms that you frequent can be kept at a toasty 72 degrees or higher. As a result of increased heating costs, and of course because of aesthetic concerns, room heaters are gaining in popularity as a home upgrade.

What Are Your Options?

Sometimes it is possible to close off or limit the ducts to certain rooms to control the heat from a central heater. The simplest way to do this is to close the registers in rooms not regularly heated. However, this means that the central heater is still being used frequently and while there are some savings, they are usually marginal.

Note: some systems come with built-in partitions. This is often the case when circulating water is used for heating. You can simply close off an area by closing the valve. It can be a highly efficient way of reducing heating costs.

Another method is to plug-in or custom install electric heating units in certain rooms. Certainly electric is the most expensive and least efficient way to heat. However, it can become practical when you only need a single heater for a small area. Using electric heating is often the least expensive method to install.

One alternative that has become increasingly popular is the natural gas or propane radiant heater. These are now made by a host of companies and approved by nearly all building departments. (I use these myself.) They rarely use fans, instead radiating heat off of a metal and glass body. (They often have glass doors that are specially treated to withstand extremely high temperatures—don't get burned by touching the glass when one of these is on!)

These heaters come in a variety of designs and shapes. They can function as inserts in fireplaces or stand alone. They can appear as a modern appliance, or what I prefer, an antique wood heater from the turn of the century. (Of course, they burn gas.)

Modern room gas heaters typically have double-walled pipe. The pipe leading to the heater has two areas. The central area is where exhaust gases are directed outside. The outer area, which surrounds the inner exhaust area, brings in fresh air from outside for combustion. As a result, these heaters can be used in closed spaces, such as bedrooms, because they do not use up the air in the room.

TRAP—WATCH OUT FOR CARBON MONOXIDE

Be wary of heaters that rely on room air for combustion, particularly in confined spaces. They can be a safety and health hazard. Carbon monoxide (an ordorless, colorless gas that can cause death) detectors are now readily available and you should seriously considered using them.

It's usually easy to connect these heaters to a thermostat, which turns them on and off, thus regulating the heat in the area.

Other options include wood burning stoves. These are now heavily regulated by the EPA and must be very efficient (in the neighborhood of 70 percent or better) to be sold.

TRAP—BE WARY OF OLD WOOD BURNING STOVES

Be wary of buying an old secondhand wood stove that might be far less efficient and that might produce toxic gases. Most older wood burning stoves must be destroyed rather than resold.

The problem with wood burning stoves is that they require lugging in wood, which often makes a mess. They are also hard to regulate, often getting so hot they drive people out of the room, or taking forever to warm up while the room remains cold.

One answer that was popular a few years ago was the pellet stove. Instead of burning wood, this stove burnt small pellets. However, in order to operate, it required an electric fan and motor. And the cost of pellets, along with other fuels, has risen dramatically. Hence, in many areas pellet stoves no longer enjoy the popularity they once had.

What Are the Typical Costs?

Electric heaters are quite inexpensive. You can often buy a room heater that plugs into a wall outlet for less than $50. However, to have them wired into a home can be quite expensive, often costing upwards of $500 per room or more.

Natural gas or propane radiant heaters usually require no separate electric outlet to function (unless you go for the optional fan that comes with many of them). However, you must have a gas outlet nearby. The stoves themselves start at around $1200 and go up from there, depending on how large and fashionable you want them to be; $2000 should buy you a good stove.

Keep in mind, however, that there is installation. Putting in a flue and dragging in a gas line can cost as much as a $1000 or more, depending on the difficulty of the installation.

TIP—EASY VENTING

Some of these gas radiant heaters can vent directly to the outside from the back (called a "direct vent"). These do not require a long flue leading up and through the chimney, which can save a lot on installation expenses.

Wood burning stoves can be costly. They typically start at around $1200 and run up to as much as $3000, depending on the size and style. They are made of heavy metal either welded or, in the case of cast iron, fitted and glued. While there are proponents of either approach, I find that both work very well.

Pellet stoves are slightly more expensive than wood stoves on the lower priced end. Keep in mind that you'll also need a storage place for the pellets as well as an electrical connection to make them operate.

What Are You Likely to Recoup?

Generally speaking, you would only install one of these heaters in an area of extreme cold weather such as the northern tier of states. In this area, more people are familiar with room heaters and are willing to pay more for a home that has them. Indeed, they will often subtract from the price if your home doesn't have one, or if your home has an old version that needs to be upgraded.

Further, many states and utilities offer significant rebates when you upgrade to a new room heater. Sometimes you recoup as much as a third to a half of the cost of the appliance through rebates! (Check with your utility companies and your county environmental control agency.)

In terms of the price at sale, you might hope to get as much as a half to the full price of the cost of a new room heater when you sell. Of course, if you hit a buyer who really knows about and likes these, the value could be much greater.

New Central Heat/Air

You can reasonably expect the central heating/air conditioning system of a home to last at least 20 years. Many systems last far longer.

If they break, however, you will be faced with repairing or replacing them. At that time, or when you feel they are inadequate or inefficient, you might want to upgrade them. Today, there are a host of new systems that, though expensive, do a much better job than any of the older systems did.

**TIP—SOMETIMES IT
JUST NEEDS A NEW
BATTERY OR FUSE**

Sometimes when your heater or air conditioner won't come on, it's not because it's broken. It's because the thermostat might need a new battery (some thermostats use them), or the fuses on the air conditioner are old and blown. Be sure to have these checked by a professional first before replacing the whole system! *(Never work on an electrical system with the power on.)*

Before you opt to replace a system because it's broken, consider the cost of repairing it. With air conditioning, there are usually two things that go wrong (besides the fuses noted above). Either the compressor is shot, demanding that you repair or replace the entire system. Or the copper tubing leading between the compressor and the coil is leaking, as is often the case with older systems, which contained screw-on fittings instead of soldered ones. In this case, the symptom is usually that the air blows but is not cold. Soldering the pipes for a few hundred dollars and pressurizing the system is often the only repair needed.

With blower type heating systems, often what goes wrong with older furnaces is that a thermocouple or thermopile will go out. These are devices that generate energy from heat and let your system know that the pilot (most modern systems do NOT use pilot lights but instead are self-igniting) is lit so that the burners can be activated. They also provide minute amounts of electricity to run your thermostat.

Replacement cost is minimal and easily done by a professional. On the other hand, if you're told that your heat exchanger (which transfers heat from the burners to air that's fed into your rooms) is shot, then by all means have the entire furnace replaced. It's almost cheaper to do that than to have the heat exchanger replaced, if a replacement could even be found.

TRAP—LEAKING HEAT EXCHANGERS CAN BE DANGEROUS

Don't use a furnace with a bad heat exchanger. Toxic exhaust fumes could be introduced in your home's air. On the other hand, because of the cost of replacement, you might want a second professional opinion that your heat exchanger is indeed shot.

If you are faced with replacing a heating/air system, be sure you do your homework and check out what's available. Today's new systems are so efficient that they could save you the entire cost of replacement in lower heating bills over the course of just a few years!

What Are Your Options?

There are about a dozen manufacturers of whole house heating/air systems. These include common names such as:

- Amana
- American Standard
- Carrier
- Lennox
- Rheem
- Trane

You might want to check a rating service such as *Consumer Reports* for the latest information on these and other manufacturers. My own preference is for Trane/American Standard.

In the old days a few decades ago, you simply bought a heater and air conditioning system and that was that. Today, your options include single state or double stage, SEER (Seasonal Energy Efficiency Rating) ratings, and more.

My suggestion is that you opt for a two-stage heater, if available. Here the heater's fan and heating system operate at two different levels. One is full blast, to heat your home up when it's cold. The other is at very low-level, to keep it warm.

Besides being superefficient, the two-stage heater overcomes what in my opinion is the single biggest drawback with thermostatically controlled fan heaters—temperature variation. Perhaps you're familiar with this. You set the temperature at 72 degrees. The heater comes on and pushes the temperature up to about 74 degrees, then shuts off. When the temp drops down to 70, it comes on again and pushes it back up to 74 degrees. As a result, you never have a true even temperature in your home. Rather, the temp is always rising and falling by around 4 or 5 degrees.

A two-stage furnace can solve this problem. Assuming it's large enough to heat your home, it will keep the temp locked right in within a degree of what you set it. Set the temp at 72, and it will stay right there!

With air conditioners, the two big items to look for is first a high SEER number and second a TXV (thermal expansion device). The SEER number tells you the efficiency of the air conditioner. Twenty-five years ago, SEERs of 5 and 6 were common. Even 15 years ago SEERs of 8 and 9 were frequently found.

Today's units, however, have SEERs ratings of as high as 15 and more. Many building departments require a minimum of a 12 SEER. EPA ratings might require higher numbers in the future.

The TXV is a special valve that helps the air conditioner arrive at and maintain efficiency. Check to be sure your selected unit has it.

Air conditioning systems also often come as single or two-stage. However, my own feeling is that a single stage with air conditioning is probably okay—it's not as crucial to have a two-stage, here.

Note: in dryer areas of the southwest, "swamp coolers" or evaporative air coolers are commonly used. These cool the air by circulating it through wet filters. These systems are effective in cutting the temperature. However, they add humidity to the home. In very dry climates this can be a plus. In most areas, however, it leads to mold and other undesirable fungus growth.

What Are the Typical Costs?

As you investigate these systems, keep in mind that the industry leaders of a few years ago might no longer hold that position today. It's a highly competitive field and companies are constantly coming up with improvements and upgrades that make their products better.

A simple gas furnace heating system (two-stage) of 80,000 BTUs suitable for a well-insulated home of about 1800 square feet can cost around $2000 to $3000 installed, depending on brand and difficulty of installation.

The cost for an air conditioner of three or four tons (each ton is equal to 12,000 BTUs) again suitable for a home of around 1800 square feet will cost around $1500 to $2500 installed. Note, "installed" means that you've already got a similar unit in place, not that you need to run all new duct work as if it were a new house installation. Add several thousands more if you need all new duct-work.

What Are You Likely to Recoup?

Unfortunately, the news here is not good. You're unlikely to recoup much if anything from replacing your whole house heater/air conditioning system when it's time to sell. Buyers might indeed be impressed by the fact that you have a new, high efficiency system that will save them money. But don't expect them to translate that into a higher purchase offer.

Generally speaking, buyers expect a modern house to have both heating and air conditioning. If you have it and it works, that's all that they require. If it doesn't work, or you don't have it, they'll subtract something from their offer. If you've got a better, newer system, they might offer you a bit more, but don't count on it.

On the other hand, in areas of extreme temperature, people will pay more if you can tell them you have a superefficient heater or air conditioner. It's possible they might pay as much as 5 percent or more for the property because of this.

New Insulation

Older homes tend to be poorly insulated. Indeed, in the southwest where the temperatures often reach more than 100 degrees in summer, some older homes have no insulation at all! Rather, they relied on now expensive air conditioning to cool them off.

Lack of adequate insulation can drive heating and cooling bills through the roof. Indeed, trying to heat or cool an uninsulated home is much like trying to do this to the great outdoors—hopeless! Heating and cooling bills under such conditions become prohibitively high.

Most homes, however, have some insulation. The real question is do you need to upgrade by adding more?

What Are Your Options?

The simplest upgrade is to add weather stripping around doors and windows. (Of course, if you add new doors and windows as noted above, they will already come weather-stripped.) This can usually be applied by an owner and, if the home had large openings that let outdoor winds in, will cut down on heating and cooling costs.

The next best upgrade is to add insulation to your attic, assuming you have one. This can be blown in and is usually quite effective in cutting heating/cooling costs. You should check to see if your attic has insulation already. If it has less than about 3 or 4 inches, new blown-in insulation should be helpful.

TRAP—COVER THE ENTIRE ATTIC

Some attic insulation companies only blow the insulation in around the attic entrance. It never gets to far areas and under eaves. This leaves the edges of your home unprotected. Be sure that you use a professional service that covers the entire attic area.

The insulation that's used today is typically made of fiberglass, although rockwool and other insulators are used. It should contain no asbestos and should be highly insulating. Ask for the R-rating. A minimum of R-11 is typical for attics, although a rating as high as R-36 is used in extremely cold conditions.

After your attic, your next best insulation option is probably to upgrade your windows, as noted earlier. After that, you might want to consider the walls. If the walls in your home weren't insulated

during construction, you can expect that there will be heat loss
through them.

Retrofitting walls for insulation is a difficult, costly, and question-
able practice. A variety of methods have been tried, including cutting holes in the walls and blowing insulation in. However, because
the walls typically have studs (wooden or metal supports) every 16
inches or so, a great number of holes must be cut. These, then, must
be covered, plastered, or otherwise fixed and painted.

Another option is to place a layer of rigid insulation perhaps an
inch thick on either the inside or outside of the walls and then frame
in a new wall covering. Again, this is a very expensive procedure. My
own feeling is that if your home doesn't have wall insulation, do the
best you can with attic and windows and simply live with it.

What Are the Typical Costs?

You can typically have insulation for a whole house of around 2000
square feet blown in the attic for around $1000, often far under. The
insulation itself is fairly cheap and the blowing process can often be
done in a few hours.

If you have a large attic, you can also have someone (or yourself,
if you're careful and wear adequate protection) lay insulation
between the ceiling joists. However, this is very difficult to do on a
house that's completed. The insulation itself is nasty, causing irrita-
tion to eyes, lungs, and skin. And there's always a chance that if
you're not careful, you'll step right through the Sheetrock ceiling!

Adding insulation to walls is usually prohibitively expensive. If
you're determined to do this, call several companies in your area
that specialize in it for bids. My own feeling is that adding interior
rigid insulation to walls, then putting in new drywall, retaping, retexturing, and repainting is the best way to go.

What Are You Likely to Recoup?

Once again, buyers are likely to be unsympathetic when you tell
them that you've spent a lot of money on insulation. They will
undoubtedly be delighted to hear it because they know it will save
them money on heating and cooling costs. But they'll probably just
consider it another plus in favor of making an offer on your home.
They're unlikely to offer you more money for it.

However, don't feel bad. Upgrading the insulation will save you plenty of heating and cooling bucks. And you'll enjoy a warmer, more pleasant indoor climate in winter and a cooler one in summer because of it.

One of the first things I check when I move into a new home is the insulation, and if it's inadequate, I immediately have more blown into the attic. I also check the weather stripping of doors and windows. I just figure it's something I need to do.

Once again, in areas of extreme temperatures, the above rules might not apply. Buyers might indeed be willing to pay several percent more for the house knowing they'll save that money on utility bills down the road.

New Fireplace Surround

One of the things that tends to date a home is the fireplace surround. The "surround" is exactly what it says it is. It refers to how a fireplace is set off from the wall in which it is located (or what surrounds it if it is freestanding).

Fireplace surrounds have changed over the years. Going back to Victorian times they were frequently made of metal, typically cast iron or stone, usually marble. In the 1950s, red brick and various flat stones were commonly used. More recently wood, tile, and granite surrounds have become popular.

It's important to understand that usually the fireplace surround's appeal is strictly a matter of personal choice. What you might like, another person might hate—and vice versa. The surround is mostly aesthetic; it doesn't add to the efficiency of the fireplace.

On the other hand, sometimes the surround will need repair. Stones or brick might have come loose or become stained. Wood might have paint chipping. Tiles might be broken. If this is the case, then you'll certainly want to fix it. While the surround's condition probably won't have much effect on the fireplace's usefulness, it will make a difference to those in the room looking at it.

What Are Your Options?

Assuming you're not putting in a new fireplace (a costly and usually unwise adventure in an existing home), your choices are to fix the existing fireplace surround or put in a new one.

If you like the existing surround, my suggestion is that you opt to fix it. The repair costs usually are not too high (see below), and the results can rejuvenate the room's appearance.

TRAP—BE WARY OF FINDING EXACT REPLACEMENTS

 A big problem with repairing old surrounds is finding replacements for old materials. The tile, wood, or bricks used in the original surround might no longer be available. Or replacements might be the wrong size, color, or design.

Replacing the surround with a totally new one, on the other hand, has never been easier. Building supply stores sell mantelpieces and surrounds that you can install yourself. All sorts of cool new materials from granite to synthetic marble to river rocks to stained wood are available. If you're unhappy with your existing surround, why not put one in that suits your pleasure?

What Are the Typical Costs?

Interestingly, repairing an old surround can often cost more than simply replacing it with a new one. The reason is that finding old materials to fit can be costly, as can the time and skill required by workmen to do the job right.

On the other hand, wood mantelpieces and surrounds available from building supply stores often cost only a few hundred dollars and can be easily stained or painted and then installed in only a few minutes.

Of course, as you get into more costly materials, such as granite, the price can soar to thousands of dollars. This is a case of getting bids and deciding how much you can and want to spend. *Be careful that the surround doesn't get in the way of the fireplace operation, or else you could cause a fire.*

What Are You Likely to Recoup?

Again, any buyer is simply going to assume that your fireplace comes with a surround that's not broken, but in good repair. Thus fixing an existing surround isn't likely to get you anything more on a sale. It simply means that the buyers won't demand that it be fixed as a condition of buying your home.

On the other hand, installing a new and "breathtaking" surround, can add appeal to your home and, like new doors, change a buyer's perspective of the value of your home. From just average, it can contribute to buyers perceiving your property as being of higher quality. And this can result in a higher price. Thus it's conceivable that if you add just the right new quality surround to your fireplace, you could recoup its value and more in a higher price that a buyer is willing to pay for a perceived higher quality home. The bottom line, of course, is that unless you're very good at interior design (or have excellent professional help), getting an increased value is almost impossible to predict.

New Kitchen Appliances

Nothing is more important to most people than the home's kitchen. And nothing dates a home faster than to have old-fashioned kitchen appliances. Unfortunately, with the heavy spate of remodeling that's occurred over the past few years, nothing has changed quicker than the appearance and quality of kitchen appliances. Thus, even if your new home is only 10 years old or less, you might discover that its kitchen appliances are obsolete. Should you upgrade them?

That depends on your own tastes. If you don't plan on selling the home, my suggestion is that you live with what you've got as long as possible. The reason is that tastes in kitchen appliances are rapidly changing. What is considered "in" today, might be out tomorrow, by the time you're ready to sell. If you can stand what you've got, keep it. Then you can remodel later on when it's closer to the time you'll want to sell.

On the other hand, many new owners simply can't tolerate what they've currently got in their kitchen. This feeling is heightened when they tour an appliance store and see all of the new items that are available. If you can't live with it, then by all means change it.

What Are Your Options?

The sky's the limit here. Recently, industrial-looking appliances were all the rage. This meant a lot of stainless steel, stoves with six gas burners, and ovens capable of baking anything from multiple turkeys to pizzas. Stainless steel sinks were also "in," as were stainless steel drums in dishwashers. In short, the kitchen of the day tended to look institutional, as if it really belonged in a large restaurant where half-a dozen chefs and helpers toiled long hours.

The rub, of course, is that most of us are spending less time in the kitchen. The modern family typically eats out more, or brings home fast food. Less and less time is being spent in the kitchen, even as the ability of kitchens to produce vast quantities of food has increased.

This paradox has not been lost on new owners who of late have begun questioning the industrial-looking kitchen. Today, a more modern approach involves smaller appliances that are increasingly efficient. While gas stoves remain the rage, electric convection ovens are also a big hit. And appliances are often in subdued colors (though not the olive green of the 1980s!). The heavy use of tile mixed with granite on countertops has led to colored sinks, often in very dark colors such as black and brown.

The new goal with dishwashers seems to be that they should not be seen or heard. They are often hidden behind a paneled façade that gives them the appearance of a cabinet. And supersilent washing is heavily marketed by manufacturers (though in truth, even the most expensive still tend to make a bit of noise).

My own suggestion is that if you're considering new kitchen appliances, you stop and consider a whole kitchen makeover. This would include new cabinets, countertops, lighting, and paint. Unless your kitchen is already quite modern, you might find that simply changing out the appliances only makes the rest of your kitchen look tattered and old.

What Are the Typical Costs?

The news, here, is not good. The cost of appliances, particularly stylish ones, has skyrocketed. Five years ago you could get a perfectly acceptable freestanding stove/oven for $350. Today, expect to pay $1000 or more.

A supersilent dishwasher might easily cost $2500. Even a conventional model can easily be more than $1000. Of course, you can also buy a starter one for around $250, but don't expect good looks or truly silent operation.

TRAP—DON'T GET HOOKED ON GADGETS

When buying appliances, be wary of manufacturers who throw in all sorts of electronics from TV screens on refrigerators to dozens of cycles on dishwashers. These days, electronics are cheap. On the other hand, making a refrigerator energy efficient or a dishwasher silent is costly. Look for what you really want from an appliance, not what a manufacturer wants to sell you.

A stand-alone refrigerator can easily cost $1200. However, if you get a unit like a Sub-Zero that's built-in, the price can jump to $3000 and much more.

A new simple white Kohler sink can run about $100. However, a stylish, colored Kohler sink can cost more than $1000.

As noted, a low-end dishwasher can run $250. A metal-lined top-of-the-line unit can cost $2500. And so on. In short, you tend to get what you pay for in terms of kitchen appliances.

What Are You Likely to Recoup?

If there's any one area of the home where you are likely to get your money back when upgrading, it's the kitchen. As noted, it tends to be the most important room of the house to most buyers—and they are often willing to pay more for an upgraded kitchen.

On the other hand, the cost of upgrading a kitchen can also be very expensive. Simply replacing the existing appliances with top-of-the-line units can easily cost $10,000. A whole kitchen makeover can cost $50,000 to $70,000.

If you spend this kind of money, don't expect to recoup it all when you sell. Indeed, if you get half to two-thirds of the expenditure back on sale, consider yourself fortunate.

On the other hand, if you're more modest in your approach, you might expect to get a better return. A $15,000 whole kitchen makeover, if done cleverly, might yield a 100 percent or more return on your investment. See also Chapter 3.

A lot, of course, will depend on what's there now. If your existing kitchen is a dog, then it will detract from the price of your home when you sell. Simply putting in a new and modern kitchen will bring the price back up to where it should be. Thus, the return of putting in the kitchen might be more easily justified.

New Roof

Upgrading the roof on your new home can only be considered a major undertaking. The reasons for doing it usually involve problems with the existing roof and these almost always involve leaks. (Some people do replace their roofs for aesthetic reasons, going for a different material or color, but that's unusual.)

My own suggestion is that you put off upgrading your roof for as long as possible. Instead of spending a large amount of money on a replacement roof, repeatedly spend a small amount of money on fixing the leaks. I would suggest replacing only when it's worn out, when it's gone beyond its normal life expectancy.

The reason, of course, is the cost of putting on a new roof, outlined below. Further, if a roof is still in good shape overall, it's often very possible to fix leaks. Indeed, many times these are caused not by holes in the roof itself, but rather by improper installation of flashing at valleys, ridges, and other roof areas.

Get bids from a variety of roofing companies that include both fixing the leaks as well as replacing the roof. Keep in mind that it's usually to the roofing contractor's advantage to put on a new roof—a major job. Fixing a leak on a roof is usually just a small job, and one that roofers don't like to undertake. The reason, simply, is that sometimes leaks are hard to fix and the roofer gets called back time and again to handle the same problem, often without being able to charge for the repeat calls.

TRAP—BE WARY
OF WEIGHT

Roofs are designed for specific weight loads. In snow country, for example, roofs can often withstand loads of 100 to 200 pounds per square foot. In warmer climes, loads of only 40 pounds per square foot might be common. The danger arises when changing a roof from lightweight (wood or tar and gravel) to heavyweight such as tile. The wood supporting the roof might not be structurally capable of withstanding the additional load. Be sure to get a structural engineering report. You might need to have the supports shored up before installing the new roof. There have been cases of roofs collapsing because too heavy a load was placed on them.

What Are Your Options?

When replacing a roof, you have an enormous number of options. These include:

- Wood shingle—(Now often in disrepute both because of its cost and its susceptibility to burning.)

- Fiberglass/asphalt shingle— (Available in many colors, styles, and lifespans—it's usually rated in how long it will last: 10, 15, 20, and more years.)

- Gravel and tar—Commonly found in the southwest and used almost exclusively on flat roofs.

- Ceramic tile—Gives a wonderful appearance and if installed correctly can last almost indefinitely.

- Metal—Comes in a variety of colors, but can be noisy in heavy rainfall and tends to look bad when dented by falling branches.

- Cement shingle—Mimics some kinds of tiles. Comes in a variety of colors and styles and has an almost indefinite life span.

- Synthetic shingle—Made from a variety of materials. Comes in a variety of colors and styles.

As noted above, be sure to choose a roof that's appropriate for the maximum load capability of your house.

What Are the Typical Costs?

Costs vary depending on your location in the country, labor costs for installation, the size of your roof, and how busy roofing contractors happen to be at the time. Prices given below include installation for a typical 2000-square–foot, double-story home.

- Wood shingle—Increasingly expensive as wood costs rise. Now available usually only in light- and medium-weight shake. Expect a lightweight shake roof to cost $7000 to $10,000.
- Fiberglass/asphalt shingle—Amongst the least expensive. Can have an entire roof installed for as little as $3500, though prices will often be higher.
- Rock and tar—Probably the least expensive. The cost could be as low as $2000.
- Ceramic tile—Usually the most expensive. Expect to pay $15,000 to $25,000, depending on the grade of tile selected.
- Metal—Medium priced roof. Expect to pay $7000 to $15,000.
- Cement shingle—A more expensive roof, but less costly than ceramic. $10,000 to $18,000.
- Synthetic shingle—Price varies greatly according to the type of material selected.

What Are You Likely to Recoup?

You're probably not going to recoup much if anything from the cost of putting on a new roof. If you change from an inexpensive roof, such as fiberglass/asphalt to tile, the upgrade will make a difference and you'll probably get some boost in the price of the home.

The problem is that everyone expects to have a house with a roof that doesn't leak. If it leaks, the owner/seller is expected to fix it. How that fix is made usually doesn't concern potential buyers, unless it doesn't work or it looks bad.

Beyond that, most buyers really aren't that interested in roofs. And, as a consequence, they aren't prepared to pay more for a newer or better one.

Look at roof replacement as a cost of living in your home. Hopefully, it isn't something you'll need to do anytime soon after you move in.

New Wall-to-Wall Carpeting

Many new owners want to replace the wall-to-wall carpeting soon after they move into a home because of cleanliness issues. After all, you really don't know what went on in the home before you bought it. There could have been pets dragging dirt in. The previous owners might never have cleaned their shoes. And if you have children that tend to play on the carpeting, you want it to be clean. Further, the carpeting might have marks and stains on it.

The easiest and quickest solution, of course, is to clean the carpeting. Carpet cleaning services will do an entire home for a few hundred dollars. And the cleaning can be effective, although it will never be as good as when you put your clothes in a washing machine.

Another reason for replacing upgrading carpeting is because you don't like the color or style. It might not match your furnishings, or new wall coverings.

Finally, the old carpeting might simply be worn out. The nap might show, there might be flattened areas, particularly where traffic is heaviest, and the strands might be starting to come out.

All of which is to say that you might find that shortly after you move in, you will want to replace the existing wall-to-wall carpeting. The big issue now is, should you replace to the existing quality or upgrade?

**TIP—ANY NEW
CARPETING LOOKS
GOOD, INITIALLY**

Keep in mind that almost any grade of carpeting you get will look good for the first six months. However, after that only high-quality carpeting will continue to look good over the years.

What Are Your Options?

Today there are almost unlimited options when it comes to wall-to-wall carpeting. There are thin–nap, commercial-style carpets that offer a hard feel but will last a long time. There are the plushes, which were popular in the recent past. There are the wool and synthetic Berbers (as well as cut-Berber), which are increasingly popular today. There are short shags (not the long shags of 50 years ago). There are multilevel carpets with and without patterns. And as for colors and textures, the sky's the limit. Just walk into any carpet store and prepare to be overwhelmed.

Keep in mind, however, that a lot of the appeal of a carpet comes from its feel underfoot, and that's determined in large part by the padding. Often an inexpensive carpeting with a thick pad will feel better than an expensive carpet with a thin pad. Of course, often the choice to replace and upgrade comes down to how much you're willing to spend.

What Are the Typical Costs?

Carpeting is sold by the square yard (9 square feet). However, it would be a mistake to simply measure the square footage of your home, divide by 9, and assume that's how many square feet of carpeting you need. While that would give you a rough figure, it would probably be off by a substantial amount.

The reason is that the amount of carpeting required for a home or a room or any area includes a substantial amount of waste. Carpeting normally can only be laid in one direction, meaning that there will be side and end pieces lost. And usually you'll want to avoid seams wherever possible, again indicating waste. As a result, you might often need as much as 10 to 20 percent more carpeting that simply measuring your home's square footage would indicate. A good carpet estimator can give you a highly accurate figure.

When you're in the carpet store, it's a good idea to get the price of the carpeting *not including installation*. The reason is that installation is often a set figure regardless of the price of the carpeting. (It can be more costly, of course, if the carpet you select is more difficult to install, there are stairs, or other problem installation areas.)

The price will vary with a low of around $15 per square yard to a high of around $60. Of course, there are the extremes. You can get low-pile carpeting down as low as $6 a yard. And at the other end of the scale, some very exquisite carpeting can cost well over $100 a square yard.

A typical price for carpeting is around $15 to $25 a yard. Add another $5 to $7 per yard for installation and padding. For a 2000-square-foot home (excluding kitchen, baths, entree, utility rooms, and so on) that requires about 200 yards, the price is typically around $3500 at the low end to $10,000 or more at the high end.

What Are You Likely to Recoup?

There are as many opinions here as there are people offering them. My own opinion is that when you decide to sell, assuming you recently put in the carpeting, typically you'll get back about half of its cost. On the other hand, if the existing carpeting is worn and truly looks bad, you stand to get back the entire price of the carpeting and maybe even more.

The reason is that carpeting is such an important element in the overall appearance of your home. Most buyers tend to look down when they walk through a home. That's only natural because most of us don't want to stumble and fall over something on the floor.

However, as a result, people see mostly floors when they tour a home. If the carpet looks terrific, if it's clean and of apparent high quality, it will make a big difference. Indeed, I've seen homes that wouldn't sell for months on end. Then the sellers put in new carpeting, raised the price of the home to accommodate the carpet's price, only to have the home sell almost immediately for full price. One can only conclude that the new carpeting made the difference.

TRAP—CARPETING AGES FAST

Don't be under the mistaken belief that you can put in new carpeting now, enjoy it for the next 10 years, and then get its value back when you sell. In 10 years' time, chances are you'll need new carpeting, again! If you upgrade your carpeting and don't plan to sell, understand that you're doing it to please yourself and you'll likely not recoup any of its cost. On the other hand, if

you plan to sell within six months of installing new carpeting, then you might very well recoup a portion of
the cost.

New Skylights

Natural lighting is an important part of every home. However,
many homes are poorly designed so that there are dark areas.
These typically occur in hallways, but they can occur in any part of
any room.

The worst examples of bad lighting typically occur in condomini-
ums and co-ops. This is because these shared living units are often
stacked with other units on their sides. This means that while a single-family home can have windows on all four sides, a typical
condo/co-op only has windows on two sides, front and back. The
other sides are actually the walls of adjoining units.

One solution to adding more natural light is to add skylights.
These can be strategically placed to bring the light of outside to
dark indoor areas. Of course, using a skylight implies you have
access to the sky. In a single story home, whether single-family or
condo/co-op (commonly called a townhouse), this is no problem.
On the other hand, if you have one or more floors above you, it can
be an insolvable problem. (Sometimes light can be directed in from
the sides, but that presents other often insolvable problems.) Thus,
skylights are usually only for single-story or top-story homes.

What Are Your Options?

There are a variety of skylight options available today. These include:

- Sealed skylights—they let in light, but no air.
- Opening skylights—they let in light and air.
- Tubular skylights—they let in light but do not allow you to see out.
- Self-installed skylights—Usually of vinyl or fiberglass construction.

Many skylights also come with some sort of shading device so that
you can opt to close out the light if it gets too intense.

What Are the Typical Costs?

It's important to understand that every home offers unique construction concerns with regard to skylights. Homes with tile roofs, for example, can be extremely costly to retrofit with skylights because many tiles are often broken in the installation.

Homes with tall attics, though unused, require framing in an area to transmit the light from the roof down through the attic to the ceiling, again an additional cost. You also will need to obtain a building permit and submit plans before having a skylight installed, and this will entail additional costs.

The cost of materials for a skylight vary depending on the quality of the product and its size. At the low end, a vinyl unit with plastic covering can cost less than $250. A glass unit that opens and closes and comes with a shade can easily cost $1000. Installation is extra.

Tubular units, which are nothing more than a glass ball at the top, a reflecting tube, and a diffuser at the bottom, are sometimes only available with professional installation and can cost anywhere from $300 to $900 per tube.

What Are You Likely to Recoup?

The amount you're likely to recoup is impossible to nail down. On the one hand, if you ask 10 buyers how much more they are likely to pay for a home with a skylight, 9 would probably say, "Not a dime more." (The 10th might come up with a figure of 50 bucks.)

On the other hand, the amount that added natural lighting will increase the perception of value in a house is likely to be significant. Homes with dark areas in rooms are simply not attractive and are likely to draw fewer and lower bids. Well-lit homes with natural light are more attractive and tend to draw better offers.

As with other optional upgrades, if you put it in, do it to please yourself. The long-term value added, if any, is simply a plus down the road.

New Lighting

While natural lighting is usually best, artificial lighting can go a long way toward making your home more attractive, livable, and salable.

Dark corners can be made to shine with a new light fixture installed nearby.

Further, new lighting can make a style statement. In the distant past, the standard lighting in rooms was floor and table lamps. A few decades ago track lighting was the rage. Today, it's recessed lighting. Some new owners will install recessed lighting in every room of their house! That's probably overkill. Nevertheless, recessed lighting is frequently used in the living room, bedrooms, and kitchen areas and can be an enormous home enhancement.

While it's usually not top on most new owner's list of things to upgrade, it should go there. Nothing will improve a home more quickly than to upgrade its lighting.

What Are Your Options?

We've already touched on these. Currently the most popular is recessed lighting. Here a "can" is attached to a beam in an attic (or ceiling crawl space) with an opening to the room below. A light (spot or regular) is inserted and sometimes a glass or plastic shade. The light is regulated by a wall switch. Typically you'll need many recessed lights in a room in order to fill it with light.

Another option is track lighting. Here a track is mounted to the ceiling (or wall) and lights attached at appropriate places along the track. The advantage of track lighting is that the lights can be moved along the track to better aim them at where they are needed.

Spotlights are well known outside but are becoming popular (in reduced wattages) inside. Typically these are used to replace conventional ceiling lights.

Light panels are also sometimes used. Typically these have a translucent piece of plastic or glass set in a frame with either incandescent or florescent bulbs behind. These throw off a diffused light and can light up large areas.

Sometimes these panels can be made of colored and leaded glass in the tradition of Tiffany lamps. The light they produce can be colorful and a topic of discussion for everyone who sees it.

Hidden lighting can be installed behind cabinets and along ceiling lines. Typically it is florescent and can be quite effective when thrown indirectly against a wall or ceiling.

Finally, you can always upgrade the lighting in your home simply by going out and buying more light fixtures. You can find a wide assortment in modern and traditional styles at lighting stores and at most home improvement centers.

TIP—THE COLOR OF LIGHT CHANGES DEPENDING ON THE SOURCE

While the human eyes tend to see all light as white, in actual point of fact, every source of light tends to give off a different tonal color, depending on the heat generated (measured in Kelvins). See the chart below.

Lighting Tones

- Outdoor sunlight—Blue
- Tungsten—Yellowish brown
- Florescent—Green
- Mercury vapor—Yellow

TRAP—COLORS CAN WARM OR COOL A ROOM

Although your brain will tell you it's all white, your mind will subtly keep you aware of the shade of light you're in. That's why commercial stores tend to have a cold look—it's the greenish cast given off by the florescent light. On the other hand, homes lit by tungsten lights tend to have a warm tinge, because of their yellowish brown cast. It's something to consider when buying lighting.

What Are the Typical Costs?

While most types of lighting are available fairly inexpensively, the cost of retrofitting can be extremely costly. For example, for around $15 you can buy a recessed light. Add a hood and bulb and the price can be as little as $25.

However, to cut a hole in the ceiling and anchor that light, as well as string a wire to it and then to a switch, can easily cost $500. Thus, when calculating the cost of upgrading the lighting in your home, be sure you also take into account the cost of installation. Remember, unless you do it yourself (which is probably unwise for most people), you're going to need a professional, usually an electrician. And that type of work does not come cheap.

TRAP—TURN OFF THE POWER!

If you're planning on doing any rewiring yourself, be sure the power is completely off. Also, remember that any new wiring requires a building permit and in some areas, only professionals are allowed to do this type of work.

Track lighting tends to be more expensive to purchase but less expensive to install. The reason is that it is typically installed on the surface of a ceiling. Only a single triple-stranded wire needs to lead to each track, while there must be separate wires for each recessed light. At the low end you can get track lighting for as little as $50 for two or three lights. At the high end with fashion statement lights, you can pay thousands.

TIP—LOW-VOLTAGE TRACK LIGHTING MIGHT WORK

Low-voltage track light has become fashionable. Typically, two open wires are run parallel to each other with light fixtures dangled from them. Unfortunately, their cost can be high, though the installation can be simpler and less expensive.

Light panels are no more expensive to install than any single lighting track or recessed light. However, depending on the materials, they can vary enormously in price. A 2-x-4-foot florescent lighting panel might only cost $40. However, a colored glass panel might cost $400 or more.

What Are You Likely to Recoup?

Upgraded lighting should definitely help you sell your home and secure a better price. However, as a practical matter, most buyers when asked probably won't be willing to give much if anything for more and better lights.

Thus, don't expect to be told you'll recoup much when you install upgraded lights. But yes, it will make your home more valuable. However, as elsewhere, the exact amount will be almost impossible to define.

New Electrical and Plumbing Systems

Why, you might reasonably ask, would any owner put in a new electrical or plumbing system? The answer is that the old one broke or is inadequate. In newer homes, this is almost never a problem. However, it can be a concern in older homes, particularly those more than 50 years old.

With electrical systems, two things usually happen over the years. Either the wiring insulation simply rots out and needs to be replaced. (Typically, it only rots in a few places, but because those places are hard to identify, a whole new system might be in order.) Or it was originally wired inadequately. This is typically the case in older homes where a ground wire was not run with the power wires.

A ground wire is the safety feature of an electrical system. It allows the current to run back to a safe ground, rather than through your body in an emergency.

Today, most kitchen and bath plugs and appliances require a ground wire. It's necessary for GFI (Ground Fault Interrupter) circuits to work, and these are a safety necessity whenever there is a wet area (utility room, bath, kitchen, garage, outdoors, etc.) around. A GFI circuit measures the current between the circuit and the ground wire and when an imbalance occurs (indicating you're getting a shock), it almost instantly closes down the circuit. It's one of those marvelous safety inventions that's been around for a few decades, but not long enough to be in older homes. All of which is to say that if your home doesn't have a ground wire as part of its circuitry, safety probably indicates it should be professionally installed.

In terms of plumbing, the biggest problem these days tends to come from older homes outfitted with galvanized iron pipes. These pipes tend to rust out over a period of 30 or so years and develop leaks. While a pressure patch can be put on an individual leak to temporarily control it, the only true remedy is to repipe the home.

Other problems occur when a safety device (such as a pressure valve where water enters the house is regulated to keep the pressure from getting too high, or a pressure/temperature safety value on a water heater, which opens if the heater gets too hot) has not been properly installed or malfunctions.

What Are Your Options?

As with any system, your options are to repair or to fix. With electrical, however, if the problem is that the insulation on wiring is old and falling apart, or a proper ground wire (or socket, plug, or switch) was never installed, your only real solution is to rewire.

In some cases, it might be possible to rewire only wet areas (bathrooms, kitchen, utility, garage, and so on). You should check with your local building department to see what their policy is on older houses that are improperly wired.

TRAP—TRIGGERING AN INSPECTION

If you call your building department, tell them what the problem is, and give them your name and address, they might insist on coming out and checking your house. If your electrical or plumbing system is truly bad, they might condemn your property. That usually means you can't live in it until it's properly fixed.

With leaking galvanized pipes, the only real solution is to completely repipe the house, usually with copper pipe. If you have more than two leaks in your galvanized pipes, this is probably indicated. The reason is that once the old galvanized iron pipes start to leak, they can go quickly. I've seen old pipe that had so many holes in it, it looked like Swiss cheese.

If all that's wrong is that there is no pressure valve on the house or your water heater needs a new pressure/temperature value, a plumber can likely install either of these in an hour or so.

What Are the Typical Costs?

Electrical and plumbing work is generally the most expensive you're likely to find on a house. That's because you need the services of a skilled professional.

Rewiring an entire house can easily cost between $7000 and $10,000. This is partly because in order to get the new wiring in, it will be necessary to break walls and it's costly to repair and repaint them. However, if only a couple of wet rooms need to be rewired, the cost could be considerably less.

Putting in all new copper plumbing will probably cost upwards of $10,000 or more. Again, a substantial part of the cost will be the repair work where walls were broken into in order to place new pipes. Putting in safety and pressure valves alone should not cost more than around $100 apiece.

TIP—LEAVE THE OLD IN PLACE

It's usually a mistake to take out the old wiring and old plumbing when replacing it with new. That just makes extra, expensive work. Besides, once it's disconnected, it shouldn't cause any harm. Better to simply install new next to it.

TRAP—DON'T DO IT YOURSELF

The temptation for many do-it-yourselfers is to handle rewiring and replumbing on their own. This is not to say that you can't do it successfully. It's just that the risk is high that you'll do something wrong that could cause someone to get a serious shock or could cause a leak that might cause extensive damage to carpeting, furniture, and so on. In many communities, owners are not allowed to do this kind of work. My suggestion is that unless you are a professional, you have a professional do it. *Turn off the power and the water before working on any electrical or water system.*

What Are You Likely to Recoup?

The answer here is simple—nothing.

The sad truth is that when it's time to sell, any buyer will expect the home to have a working plumbing and electrical system. He or she won't be in the least impressed that you spent $20,000 to rewire and replumb. They'll just expect it to be there and in good shape. On the other hand, if you don't do it, buyers will probably subtract the cost of doing it from the price they offer.

This is one of those situations where you don't do the work in order to make money or recoup money. You do it because you have to in order to live in the home—and to eventually sell it.

New In-Ground Pool/Spa

Many first-time homeowners dream of having a pool, or at least a spa, on their property. If they have children, they envision the kids playing in the water in the summer. They see themselves barbecuing at pool/spa parties. They look forward to quiet warm evenings with the pool light on reflecting through the blue water.

Is any of this realistic? Indeed, all of it is. It's the plus side of having a pool or spa. The problem is that there is a negative side. Upgrading to a pool or spa in a home that doesn't have one is incredibly expensive today (see below). Further, once you have a pool or spa, it requires constant upkeep.

TIP—POOLS/SPAS ARE KIND OF LIKE BOATS

I'm reminded of the old saw about boats—the best two days of your life are the day you buy one and the day you sell it. The same can be said to apply to pools and spas.

You'll need to become an expert on keeping the water clean. This means running pumps and filters and adding chemicals. You might need to buy one of the many types of pool robots that come on automatically and clean the pool each day. Alternatively, you can hire a pool company to come in and do this work for you—for a fee.

Also, the pool/spa will probably be unused a large portion of the year. Typically the first year you put it in, you'll use it all year. The second year you'll use it during the warmer months. The third year only the kids will use it. The fourth year it will remain largely unused. If you're in a colder climate, you'll need to drain and winterize it to protect it from freezing. (Freezing water can expand and ruin your pool.)

Should you get an overgrowth of algae (because you weren't caring for it carefully enough) you'll need to superchlorinate it or add harsh chemicals to get rid of this. Sometimes it will require draining the pool and acid washing it. In extreme cases you'll need to have it replastered.

Finally, you'll find that you'll need to put at least a 5-foot fence all around the pool/spa with a self-closing gate to prevent a child or other person from accidentally getting in and injuring or drowning themselves. And, because of the risk of injury or drowning, you'll find that your homeowner's liability policy can shoot up in cost. (Reread the first chapter.) All of which is to say that in-ground pools/spas are not all that wonderful. I've had many of them, and given a choice, would have none.

What Are Your Options?

You can hire a contractor who specializes in the field to build an in-ground pool and or spa for you. The work can be done in several months if the contractor works constantly at it.

However, be aware that there are permits required and in some communities these can be hard to come by. You might even be required to file a sort of environmental impact report before you're given permission to put your pool/spa in!

Of course, you could put in an above-ground pool or spa. These are made of plastic, fiberglass, and other materials. Some small ones are simply blown up. Others use a metal structure to maintain the sides. And others are made of hardier woods.

Most are considered temporary. Keep in the mind that the same constraints with regard to cleaning and liability apply. You'll need a fence, extra insurance, chemicals, pumps, filters, and so on.

What Are the Typical Costs?

This is what usually discourages most people. Twenty-five years ago you could put in a small in-ground pool for around $10,000. Today, it's probably going to start at $50,000 and go up very rapidly.

Today a nice-sized in-ground spa with tile and fountain sprays can easily cost $35,000. A small starter spa can cost $20,000. Keep in mind that you'll probably want to landscape your back yard at the same time as well as add cement decking, and the price here can easily start at $10,000 and go up. All of which is to say that spending $100,000 on a backyard pool/spa with landscaping is not unheard of.

An above-ground pool/spa, however, is a totally different matter. These start at only a few hundred dollars. For $5000 you can usually get a fairly large one including minimal equipment. Just remember, however, these tend to be temporary. And many people do find them unsightly.

What Are You Likely to Recoup?

The good news is that a pool/spa normally does add to the value of your property. The bad news is that they rarely add as much as they cost.

Realistically, you can probably expect to get 5–7 percent or more for your home because you've added a pool or spa. If you carry through the calculations, you quickly see that the more expensive a home you have, the more likely you are to recoup your money. For example, if you spend $50,000 to add a pool/spa to a home originally worth $200,000, it might only add 7 percent or $14,000 to the value.

On the other hand, if your home is worth $700,000, you add the pool/spa, and the increase is still 7 percent, the value added is $49,000, roughly the same amount as it cost you. The more expensive the property, the more sense it makes to add a pool/spa.

My own feeling is that it's usually a mistake to add a pool/spa to a home. It's costly, you'll get only minimal benefits from it over time, and when you resell, you'll have trouble getting your money out.

12

Your Home Maintenance Schedule

Just as your car has a maintenance schedule, so too does your home. The problem is that most homeowners simply aren't aware of this schedule and don't do necessary maintenance and repair. As a result, they can get into trouble when a furnace suddenly stops working or a roof develops a massive leak. Or what could be far worse, the house begins to tilt from a broken foundation.

Of course, homeowner's need to be forgiven for not keeping up their home maintenance schedule because, in nearly all cases, they are not given it! When you buy your home you get your escrow closing documents, your loan documents, sometimes your Homeowner's Association documents, even a copy of the deed showing that you own the property.

But how often have you (or has any owner, for that matter) been handed a home maintenance schedule? Unfortunately, it's one of those things that's simply doesn't exist. However, here we're going to correct the situation. Below you'll find a maintenance schedule that you can apply to your home.

It's easy to follow and easy to keep. It only asks you to check through it twice a year, once in the spring before the hot summer season hits, and once in the fall before winter's rains and snows come down. Pick two days a year. They could be the first day of spring and fall, two birthdays, or any other days that you can easily remember. Keep to this maintenance schedule and you should spend many years of trouble-free enjoyment in your home.

Home Maintenance Schedule in the Fall

☐ Drainage

If your home is located on a typical lot, it will drain to the front where the street is located. This is the standard way of grading a lot. Typically the water flows from the backyard, around the sides of the house, and out to the front. However, over the course of the summer months it's not uncommon for many homeowners to stack unwanted materials (wood, dirt, sand, toys, old appliances, and so on) along the sides of the house. Come winter rains, the water is prevented from flowing out from the back of the house by the clutter and accumulates in standing puddles. This can lead to wet basements and crawl spaces and over time can undermine a foundation.

Check to be sure the sides of your house are clear so that water can flow out to the street. If you notice that in the winter the water doesn't flow properly even when the sides drain, you might have a low spot in back. You might need to install French drains (4' plastic hoses with holes in them buried just below the soil level to accumulate water) to lead the water out. If the problem is very severe, a sump pump that goes on automatically when the water level rises might be in order. Check with a good gardener and/or soils engineer.

☐ Electric

You want to be sure that when the rains and snows come, they don't short out any wiring you might have. Check outdoor plugs to be sure they are high off the ground and nothing is leaning against them. (All outdoor plugs should be GFI to help prevent shock.) Be sure outdoor wiring and lights are well out of harm's way and that the insulation is not damaged.

Some electricians suggest tripping each circuit breaker once a year to be sure it's operating properly. I don't advocate this because there's too much chance of getting a shock.

Always be sure the power is completely off before doing any electrical work.

☐ **Garden**

You'll want to trim down roses and many other deciduous trees. Check with a good gardener for the best time to do this. Also, you might want to tie down or remove trellises, canvas patio covers, and other implements that might be damaged by snow or wind.

☐ **Gutters/Drain Spouts**

Most homeowners never realize just how important these are. While part of the function of gutters and drain spouts is to keep water off your back when entering the house or looking out the window, the major reason for having them is to protect your home's foundation.

When water runs off the roof of your house, if it falls straight down, it will tend to collect right at the base of your home, at the foundation. Water seeping under the foundation can undermine it, especially in freezing weather or where the soil is expansive.

The purpose of the gutters is to collect roof water and direct it to the drain spouts. The purpose of the drain spouts is to funnel that water down from the roof and then away from the house.

You should check to see that all gutters and drains are clear of leaves and otherwise clean. Further, it's often a good idea to extend the bottom of the drain spout several feet away from the house to be sure that rain water doesn't puddle beneath them.

☐ **Heater/Furnace**

Operating under the premise that the best time to stop a problem is before it happens, a good check of your heating system is in order. The first step is to put in a new filter. If you have a heater/air conditioner combination, you can expect the filter to be dirty from use over the summer. Putting in a new filter will not only clean up the air in the house, but will also help to reduce your heating bill by making the heater more efficient.

While you're at it, use your vacuum cleaner to clean around the heater. Often dust will accumulate there and could eventually lead to a fire. *Do not vacuum inside the heater, as you could damage it or cause a fire.*

If yours is a blower furnace, check the registers in each room. Be sure they open and close easily, or else fix or replace them.

Then, turn your heating system on just to be sure it works. Sometimes lack of use will cause a gas or oil valve to stick. Sometimes a thermocouple or thermopile (that operates the safety devices and thermostat) will fail and the heater won't come on. You'll usually need a professional to fix these.

Finally, have your heat exchanger checked. Either a professional furnace installer or a utility company person can handle this. They are looking to see that gases produced by the furnace do not mingle with clean air circulated throughout the house. This can be a deadly combination (and is a good reason to have a carbon monoxide alarm installed in the house). If your heat exchanger is malfunctioning, you probably need a new heater. The exchangers can rarely be fixed.

☐ Paint

It's a good idea to give your house a once-over look for cracked, peeling, and otherwise deteriorating paint. Besides giving your house aesthetic appeal, paint also acts to preserve the surface beneath it. If the paint is bad, water can get into wood below it and rot or crack it. If it's stucco, bad paint can actually let water pass through it (stucco is basically porous) and into the walls of your home. If you have metal, bad paint can allow water to oxidize its surface.

The remedy, of course, is to scrape off the bad paint and put on a coat of new paint.

Caution: Prior to 1978, lead paint was widely used in homes. If you have an older home, you might need to have it checked to see if it has lead paint. Do not attempt removal yourself. Scraping, sanding, or burning will only release it into the atmosphere. Use a professional lead abatement service.

☐ Roofs

Roofs only leak when it rains. Therefore you should check them before the rainy season.

Caution: Do not get on top of the roof to check it. If you climb onto the roof yourself, you stand an excellent chance of falling off and getting injured or killed. Besides, you probably won't be able to tell if there are any leaks from the top.

Instead, go into your attic opening on a sunny day and look up. If you see any light coming through, your roof leaks. If you see water stains on the roof beams, your roof leaks. Call a roofer to check it out. Look at the ceiling under your roof. If there are any water stains, you probably have a roof problem. Call a professional to check it out.

Finally, get a pair of binoculars and stand across the street and look at your roof. Are there any shingles missing? Is any of the metal flashing torn or standing away from the chimney, gutters, or valleys? Are any tiles broken? Are there lots of leaves and branches on your roof? If so, call a professional to check out and clean your roof. Again, don't get on your roof yourself. It's simply too dangerous.

☐ Water Heater

Your water heater is what supplies hot water to your home. The last thing you want is to run out of it, or to have it suddenly stop, particularly in the middle of winter.

Check out your heater. Is it leaking? If it is, it probably needs to be replaced. It could just be a bad valve, but usually a leaking water heater indicates that it has rusted out and will soon fail. Replace it.

Check out the safety pressure/temperature valve. This is usually located at the top of the heater. A drainpipe runs down the side from it and goes outside. If there is no proper drainpipe, do not check the valve, as you might be scalded by rapidly escaping hot water. Call a plumber to install a proper drain.

You check the valve by momentarily opening it. This lets hot water escape down the drain and to the outside. If it opens, the valve is working. Be aware that with older valves, the act of checking them can introduce rust and other sediments into the valve and prevent it from closing. Meaning, you'll need to call a plumber to have the valve replaced!

If you live in an area where sediments are commonly found in the water, you'll want to have your heater drained. (You'll usually know if you have sediments because they typically appear as granules of sand at the bottom of toilets and sinks.)

Water heaters have a drain stem at their bottom. A hose can be connected to it leading safely outside, and then the valve can be opened and water allowed to drain. Because the drain is at the bottom of the tank, usually the sediment will flow out first. When the water runs clean, the valve can be closed. If no water comes out (the valve is clogged with sediment), you might want to consider getting a new heater. Sediment means there's less room for water in the tank and it's heating inefficiently. *Beware of very hot water coming out of the drain.* Finally, check to be sure your water heater is properly strapped to your house to prevent movement during an earthquake.

☐ Weather Stripping

Be sure to check around all doors and windows. This is especially true in an older home. Even a small crack at a door or window can let in a huge amount of cold air, which can cause uneven heating in your home and your fuel bills to skyrocket.

Most building supply stores sell weather stripping along with instructions on installing it. But it can be tricky. You might want a handyman to do it for you.

Home Maintenance Schedule in the Spring

☐ Air Conditioner(s)

It's a good idea to check out your air conditioner before you really need it during the hot summer months. Of course, there's not a whole lot to check.

Change the filter. This will help assure that you'll get clean air in the house. It will also keep your unit working at peak efficiency.

Turn your air conditioner on. If it does not immediately come on, do not panic. The oil in many compressors accumulates in the bottom of the unit over the winter months and coagulates. Most compressors have a small coil that comes on to heat this oil and thin it when you first change the setting on your thermostat from heat to cool. However, it can take hours for the warm-up process to occur. Turn your air conditioner on and if it doesn't immediately start working, let it sit for awhile. It might begin working a few hours later.

Of course, if it never comes on, then chances are a fuse has blown or (worst case) your compressor is out. It's time to call the air conditioner repairman.

If it comes on, check to see that it's blowing cool air. Usually you can tell by feeling the air at a register. However, if you want to be precise, you can use a thermometer to measure the air at the return (where it enters the air conditioner) and at a register. At a register it should be at least 15 degrees (and as much as 20 degrees) cooler, indicating that the unit it working. If you do not get cool air, call the repairman.

Note: if you use a "swamp cooler," an evaporative cooling device, now is the time to check the water filters, clean them, and replace those that are damaged.

☐ Attic Fan

Many homes in hot climates use an attic fan in addition to an air conditioner. The attic fan helps draw in cooler outside air and evacuate hotter inside air in the attic. By cooling the attic, it can reduce the amount of work that an air conditioner has to do to cool your home.

Be sure your attic fan works. Usually there is a trip switch in the garage to test it. Also, be sure it comes on at an appropriate temperature (usually between 90 and 120 degrees). There is usually an automatic temperature switch located near the fan.

Be careful about going into the attic. If you're not sure of how to do this, get a professional to check it out. You could fall through the ceiling and get seriously injured or even killed.

☐ Carpets

As part of spring cleaning, you should clean your carpets at least once a year. Not only will this get the dirt out, but it will help reduce the number of mites that cause allergies.

Whole-house carpet cleaning is not expensive and should only cost a couple of hundred dollars at most. Be wary, however, of offers that are too cheap to be true. Usually they are and you might get someone who simply waters down the dirt in the carpets, instead of removing it.

☐ Floors

After the winter season, check your floors. Be sure that they are all still level. Watch out for any floors that slant or bulge. This could indicate a problem with the foundation or the structure of the house.

Sometimes during the winter, water will accumulate under the house and will cause stress on the floors. Now is the time to discover if this has happened and correct the problem. Your best bet is a contractor or a structural engineer.

☐ Foundation/Slab

Walk around the outside of your home and look at the foundation. You should be able to see it from the surface of the ground to where the house proper starts.

You're looking for anything unusual. In particular, look for cracks, especially those that are wider at the top than at the bottom. "V"-shaped cracks could indicate serious problems. Hairline cracks usually don't mean much, as most concrete cracks a little bit like this.

Also check for any bulges or "rotten" concrete (it looks rotten and decaying). These also indicate problems. When you detect a problem, call in a structural engineer as well as a concrete contractor. Get to the bottom of it before you house bottoms out.

☐ Garden

Now's the time to rejuvenate that yard. Get rid of trees and shrubs that died over the winter. Plant bare-root trees. Fertilize and trim as necessary. Work that's done now will pay big dividends later in the year.

☐ Kitchen

Because you use your kitchen appliances all year long, it might seem strange to put the kitchen on an annual checklist. However, there are a number of things that you might want to do in your kitchen at least once a year.

- **Touch up cabinets**—Whether stained or painted, they get nicked during the year. Why not set a time once a year where you get rid of those nicks? Also, it's a great time to wash down the cabinets as well!

- **Bleach your tile**—The grout between the tiles accumulates dirt. One way to remove it is to use a mild bleach solution. It will make your kitchen counter look better, and it could get rid of a lot of germs!

- **Seal granite**—If you have a granite countertop, it should be sealed on a regular basis. If not sealed, stains could permanently deface it. Any building supply house should sell a variety of sealants that can do the job.

- **Clean appliances**—Of course, you keep them clean on a regular basis. But why not do a deep cleaning at least once a year? Remove electric burners and catch-plates and clean. Get behind the appliances with a mop and vacuum cleaner. Wash the glass face of the oven (but only when it's cool!). Get rid of that accumulated dirt and grime.

☐ Paint

Take a quick tour of the outside of your home. Chances are the winter climate has taken its toll and there will be places where the paint has weathered. Why not take the time now to repaint and get your home ready for summer? *Caution: Prior to 1978 lead paint was widely used on home exteriors. If you have an older home, you might need to have it checked to see if it has lead paint. Do not attempt removal yourself. Scraping, sanding, or burning will only release lead paint into the atmosphere. Use a professional lead abatement service.*

It's also a good idea to take a quick tour of the interior of your home. Look particularly for handprints on walls and doors and doorjambs. Many times these can be scrubbed off. But if not, a good new coat of paint should do the trick.

☐ Pool and Spa Motors

If you have a pool and/or a spa, check the motors to be sure they are in good working condition. Some older motors need to be oiled; most new ones are permanently sealed. Any squealing or grinding noise suggests the motor is about to crash and needs repair or replacement.

Also, check your pool/spa filter. Now would be an excellent time to clean or replace it. In some pools/spas this can be a monthly chore, but in others once or twice a year will do.

You might want to handle these duties yourself. Or a good pool service will do it all for you. If you bring a bad motor into many pool supply stores, they will handle the repairing (or replacement) of it.

☐ Spiders and Insects

Usually these blossom along with the flowers in the spring. You can always call the pest control person. But if you don't like toxic (certainly to insects and perhaps to humans) sprays put around your home, you can take other steps.

Spiders require webs to survive, and most of these are found in the corners where walls and ceiling come together. Simply using a dust mop with a long handle to get rid of spider webs can be an effective way of keeping these pests out of your home.

Check your screens or doors and windows. These, too, can be very effective in keeping insects from setting up housekeeping in your home.

If ants are a problem, consider using one of the less toxic sprays around the exterior of your home. Ants live in the ground outside the home and then go inside to nibble on your food and water. Simply attack their trails and you can usually get rid of them.

Of course, if you have a serious problem, say rodents in the attic or bees in the walls, you will want to call in a professional exterminator. However, checking out your home at least once a year will help to keep pests under control.

☐ Structural Cracks

These usually occur at the corners of windows and doors. Diagonal cracks going out from a corner usually indicate some settling of the house, which is to be expected over the winter months. I've never seen a house that's more than a few years old that doesn't have some cracks in the walls.

Straight vertical or horizontal cracks nears doors and windows suggest a problem with the structure. These cracks are probably following the line of a stud or a header. These might have been installed improperly or might simply not have enough nails in them to hold them in place. You might want to get a carpenter to give you an opinion.

Most cracks in the walls are not serious. However, cracks in the ceiling, and large or plentiful cracks in the walls, might indicate a more serious problem that needs immediate attention. Check with a contractor, professional home inspector, or structural engineer.

☐ **Windows**

Finally, check your windows to be sure none have been broken by flying branches over the course of the winter. This is also an excellent time to wash them, a chore that none of us ever wants to do!

Appendix

Tips When Renovating Your Home

If you're considering upgrading your home, you should pause before you start and look around to see what others have done. Since the turn of this century, home upgrading has been skyrocketing and all sorts of resources are available to you. The following is taken from my book *Tips and Traps When Renovating Your Home* and, I believe, should prove very helpful.

Don't Reinvent the Wheel!

The worst thing you can do is to try to reinvent the wheel. Regardless of how big or small your upgrading project, don't think that you're the first person to ever attempt it. You're not. While there might be some strange new twist peculiar only to your house, in general everything that can be done in upgrading has been done by others. Benefit from their experience.

As I noted, there are a host of resources available to you before you start your project. Take a look at these and "steal" ideas from them. You might want to put a whirlpool bath in your bathroom. See how others have done it, the layout they used, how they made it fit into a small bathroom, the different styles, colors, and prices that are available. Or you might want to renovate the entire home. Check out what others have done with a home similar to yours, the clever changes they made, their use of space and light. Look into your options. Your resources today are almost limitless.

193

What about Magazines and Books?

There are a host of magazines out there today that cater to renovators (see the list at the end of this section). Many are composed entirely of plans for home design. Others concentrate on kitchen and bath, while yet others emphasize interior design.

You don't need to subscribe to or buy all of these (although you might want a subscription to one or two magazines you find particularly attuned to your needs). But you will find it helpful to peruse many of them. Sometimes just looking at the pictures will give you a new idea, something different you hadn't considered before that will solve a design problem.

TRAP—READY-MADE OFTEN ISN'T

Be careful of using the plans offered in magazines just as they are. While some might be quite complete, you usually will need to take them to an architect or draftsman to make them specific to your needs (or redraw them yourself).

TIP—A PICTURE MIGHT BE BETTER THAN ITS SUBJECT

It might seem obvious, but keep in mind that your home upgrading will never come out looking the same as the picture in the magazine. Yours will look different, perhaps better in your eyes. You're just there to get ideas, not to try to replicate exactly what you see.

(Check out "Homestyles Home Plans," 213 E. Fourth St., 4th Floor, St. Paul, MN 55101, www.homestyles.com. There are a few articles on design, but mostly different style homes with whole-house layouts.)

Should I Try Showrooms?

Every manufacturer of a home product has a showroom somewhere. Sometimes these are just one manufacturer's product. Other times they are many different manufacturers showing in groups such as kitchens or baths. The showrooms are another great place to get your ideas for what you want to do in your renovation.

The Whole House

Believe it or not, there are whole house showrooms. These are the model homes that builders offer. If you're about to do a whole house upgrade, stop, don't do another thing until you check out the model homes in your area. You will very quickly learn what's currently in style (what buyers are looking for). You might find that you want to adopt many of the new features that builders offer.

Also, check out any resales that are of similar design and age as yours, particularly if they are located in your neighborhood. You will be able to see some by simply walking in on "open houses." In other cases, a friendly real estate agent will be be happy take you by.

TIP

You needn't use a subterfuge to get the agent to show you homes—you don't need to say you're really a buyer when you're not. Just explain that you're upgrading your home and that when you're done, you'll consider reselling. That's only the truth. An agent will be delighted to show you homes in the hopes of eventually getting a listing on yours—and possibly selling you another one.

Kitchens and Baths

Showrooms are located all over. Many home centers such as Home Depot, Lowes, and others have showrooms for kitchen and bath. Retailers who specialize in the sale of kitchen and bath fixtures also will often have extensive showrooms. In addition, cabinet manufacturers will often have their own showrooms.

Your best bet is to simply check the Yellow Pages of your phone book. Look for ads under the following headings:

Bathroom cabinets and equipment

Bathtubs

Cabinets

Kitchen cabinets and equipment

Kitchen/Bathroom remodeling

Pay particular attention to advertising that says something such as, "Visit out showroom." I suggest that you call first to be sure that the showroom is open (not itself being renovated!) and has enough variety to be of interest to you.

Fixtures

Retailers specialize in a variety of home fixtures from appliances such as stoves and ovens to lighting to faucets. These retailers also have their own showrooms.

While visiting a fixture showroom is useful, it's a necessity when you get down to the nitty-gritty of finally assembling the materials for your renovation. The reason is that you'll get an idea of what's out there right then and, just as important, how much it costs. For example, you might think you can simply get a faucet assembly for your bathroom sink and tub that looks good and costs under $100 for both.

While you can get them for that price, their appearance is likely to be plain and the materials used in them might be cheap. Actually, a first-class faucet for a bathroom sink will cost in the range of $150 or more. A first-class Roman style faucet for a spa type tub could easily cost $500 and up. And that's just for the faucet, not the tub! High-quality lighting fixtures can be even more expensive. And then there's the cost of the sinks and tubs, and we're only in the bathroom! Visiting fixture showrooms will give a realistic handle on what's out there, what it costs, and even how long it takes to order.

What Are My Internet Options?

These days any business that's worth its salt has a Web site. (Check out robertirwin.com, by the way!) That includes manufacturers of virtually any product you'll need in your home renovation, from makers of cabinets to flooring manufacturers. Many local contractors also have their own Web sites. Visiting these Web sites will often allow you to see many of their newest products, get information on cost, installation, and delivery, as well as fill you with a host of new ideas. Just a few of my favorite sites include:

Generic search engines:

www.google.com

www.yahoo.com

www.excite.com

www.lycos.com

Search words that are helpful:

home or remodeling

home shows

home design

kitchen and bathroom

Search engines with links to many manufacturers of home consumer products. Look here if you want to find out who makes a sink or cabinet. Also references to contractors, associations, and architects:

www.buildingonline.com and www.build.com

Taunton Press books, tapes, and videos on virtually every area of home improvement, with the emphasis on doing it yourself:

www.taunton.com

Kohler makes a wide range of sinks and kitchen and bath fixtures and faucets:

www.kohler.com

An online showroom for faucets and other fixtures. Offers some discounted merchandise:

www.faucet.com

Diamond Cabinets, a national distributor of cabinets. Shows pictures of different cabinet styles and designs:

www.diamond2.com

Maker of high-quality kitchen cabinets:

www.kraftmaid.com

Manufacturer of cabinets sold nationwide:

www.merilat.com

Manufacturers of a wide variety of tiles used for kitchens, baths, entryways, and elsewhere:

www.daltile.come

The original home remodeling show from public television, it goes through a complete home renovation. Site contains info on many of the previous shows as well as the homes that were done and lists contractors and manufacturers used:

www.thisoldhouse.com

The Web site for the HomeTime show seen both on public television and The Learning Channel. Includes tips from the shows on virtually every aspect of home renovation. Sells videos and books:

www.homeimprovement.com

The National Association of the Remodeling Industry—contains many references to other sites as well as good tips on selecting contractors as well as doing the work yourself, including coming up with a workable design:

www.nari.org

On TV

I'm sure you've already seen many of them, but within the last few years dozens of truly excellent home renovation shows have emerged both on PBS, TLC, and other networks, from *This Old House* to *HomeTime* to many more. Don't overlook the opportunity these shows offer. They are great for both getting ideas as well as seeing how things are done. While many of the shows tend to gloss over the real how-to aspects of jobs, some go into scrupulous detail.

Of course, you can't be watching TV all the time, and chances are they won't actually be showing the very project you want to do, just when you want to do it. So check out their Web sites. Several are given above. You can usually buy tapes by specific shows as well by category of project (kitchen, bath, window, doors, etc.).

What about Checking with Designers and Architects?

It really depends on how big a project you have in mind and how thick your wallet is. Architects can give you ideas, but they are in business to create plans and designs, so you might have to pay for them.

How they typically operate is that they will want some sort of up-front fee to ensure that you are really serious about doing the work. Then they will talk with you and show you design ideas in books and magazines as well as plans and sketches of their earlier projects. When they have a good idea of what you want, they'll usually make sketches. You can see how these look and then make adjustments or changes. When everything is just as you like, they'll draw up a set of plans that any competent builder can execute.

The cost is high, but the results are usually worth it. If it's a whole house, the architect might want a percentage of the overall building costs. For smaller projects there might be a set fee or a per-hour charge. Figure on spending at least a thousand dollars and often considerably more for their services.

Designers work a little differently. Often they get some or all of their fee from the manufacturers of products that you buy. However, in some cases they, too, might also want an up-front fee (sometimes refundable after you make purchases), or an hourly fee.

Designers can take you to local "design centers," showrooms sometimes covering entire buildings where manufacturers have set up to display everything from furniture to window treatments to kitchen appliances. Sometimes designers will be able to actually save you considerable money by getting products at steep discounts and passing some of that savings along to you. Usually, however, they deal only in the better-quality items, so the prices are pretty steep to begin with.

Designers are listed in the Yellow Pages of the phone book under "Interior Design." However, you're usually better off if you can get a recommendation from a friend who has worked successfully with one. Builders, showroom salespeople, and even furniture salespeople can also often recommend designers.

Index

A

adjustable mortgages
  caps on, 32
  refinancing the mortgage and, 31–32
adjusted tax basis, 69–70
air conditioning units, 186–187. *See also*
  heating and a/c
Alternative Minimum Tax (AMT), 68
American Society of Home Inspectors
  (ASHI), 123
appearance of premises, Before You
  Move In check of, 125
appliances, 161–164
  Before You Move In check of,
    125–127
  insurance and, 6–7, 6
  Seasonal Energy Efficiency Rating
    (SEER) in, 154–155
  water heaters, 185–186
appraisers, 117–119
architects for renovations, 199–200
attic fans, 187

B

bars on windows/doors, 87–88
bathroom, 46–47, **47**
  fixtures in, 196
Before You Move In Checklist, 123–130
  appearance of premises, 125
  carpeting, 128–129
  cleanup and repairs, 128–130
  emergency response numbers, 127
  fences, 127
  fireplaces, 127
  garage, 129
  garage doors, 126
  health and safety check, 124–127
  heating and a/c, 126

Before You Move In Checklist (*Cont.*):
  improvements, 129–130
  inspections, 123–124
  locks, 127
  paint, 128
  pet odors, 128
  roof, foundation, 127
  smells, 124–125
  smoke detectors, fire extinguishers,
    127
  tie downs (earthquake regions), 127
  utilities, appliances, 125–127
  water heaters, 126
  windows and screens, 129
  wiring, rewiring, 126
black mold, 14–15
blended interest rates, second
  mortgages and, 29
building permits, renovations and, 42

C

cable modem hookups, 133
cancellation of insurance, 15–16
capital gains taxes, 70. *See also* taxes,
  selling your home and capital
  gains
  refinancing the mortgage and, 27
carbon monoxide dangers, 150
carpeting, 128–129, 167–170
  maintenance of, 187–188
ceiling renovation, "popcorn," 137–140
central air conditioning, 152–156
cleanup and repairs, Before You Move
  In check of, 128–130
commission rates, 113–114
comparative market analysis (CMA),
  104–105. *See also* current value of
  home, 104

NOTE: **Boldface** numbers indicate illustrations; *t* indicates a table.

conditions, covenants and restrictions
(CC&Rs), 52–55
credit cards, 63
credit rating, refinancing the mortgage
and, 23
current value of home, 101–119
appraisers to calculate, 117–119
asking price vs. actual price in, 112
calculation of, 102
charting, 117, **117**
commission rates and, 113–114
comparative market analysis (CMA)
in, 104–105
comparing other houses to yours in,
108–111, 109*t*
date to work from, 105
emotions vs. logic in, 106
equity value of, 116, 117*t*
estimates in, 108
fix up costs and, 114–116
flyers from real estate agents and,
103
market value and, 113
nearby sales as gauge of, 103
net value of home and, 116, 117*t*
price increases in neighborhood
and, 102
price ranges in, 111–112
reasons to know, 101–102
recent purchase price and, 103–104,
106
sales figures in, 107
title insurance and escrow costs in,
114
transaction costs figured into, 104,
113–116, 116*t*
trends in, 107–108, 112

D
deductible mortgage interest, 25,
67–68
deductible, in insurance, 16–17
depreciation, taxes and, 70
designers and architects for renovations,
199–200

disaster insurance, 11, 12
Federal Emergency Management
Agency (FEMA) and, 12
discrimination in zoning and CC&Rs, 53
do-it-yourself renovations, 42
doors, 145–148
drainage, 182
DSL hookups, 133

E
electrical systems, 175–178
maintenance of, 182
electronic security systems, 91–95
electronic sensors, window security, 89
emergency response numbers, 127
equity value of home, 116, 117*t*
escrow costs
current value of home and, 114

F
fall seasonal maintenance, 182–186
Federal Emergency Management
Agency (FEMA) and natural
disasters, 12
fences, 127
fire extinguishers, 127
fire insurance, 11
fireplace surrounds, 159–161
fireplaces, 127
fix-up costs, current value of home
and, 114–116
fixed-rate mortgages, refinancing the
mortgage and, 31–32
fixtures, 196
floors, maintenance of, 188
foundation/slab, 127
maintenance of, 188

G
garage, 129
garage doors, 126
garden maintenance, 183, 188
gutters/drain spouts, 183

H

health and safety check, Before You Move In, 124–127

heating and a/c
air conditioning units, 186–187
attic fans, 187
Before You Move In check of, 126
carbon monoxide dangers, 150
central systems for, 152–156
fireplace surrounds, 159–161
insulation, 156–159
maintenance of, 183–184
room heaters, 149–152
Seasonal Energy Efficiency Rating (SEER) in, 154–155
weather stripping, 186
wood burning stoves, 151

home appliances. *See* appliances

home businesses. *See* home office

home equity loans, 30

home improvement, 24–25, 33–49. *See also* renovations
loans for, 30
refinancing mortgage to get money for, 24–25

home office, 72–74
insurance and, 12–13
record keeping for, 75
selling your home and, 74
tax implications of, 72–74

home warranty plans, 5–6

homeowner's associations (HOA), 56
zoning changes and, 56–58

I

identify theft, 98

insects, 190

inspections, 123–124

insulation, 156–159

insurance, 3–19
agents for, selecting, 19
black mold and, 14–15
building and personal property, 10–11
cancellations, nonrenewals of, 15–16

insurance (*Cont.*):
deductible amount in, 16–17
disaster, 11, 12
Federal Emergency Management Agency (FEMA) and natural disasters, 12
fire, 11
home appliance, 6–7
home warranty plans and, 5–6
land or title, 9–10
liability limits in, 12–14
home businesses and, 12–13
pools and spas, 13
special needs (valuable possessions), 14
life, 19
loss of building, 9
need for, 3–4, 8–9
overinsurance and, 4–5, 5*t*
premium increases in, 15–16
replacement costs and, 8, 17–18
reviewing coverage in, 8
umbrella plans in, 13
underinsurance problems and, 7–8

interest rates
refinancing the mortgage and, 22–23, 26
second mortgages and, 29

Internet resources for renovations, 197–198

K

kitchen, 44–46, **45**
appliances, 161–164
fixtures in, 196
maintenance of, 188–189

L

land title insurance, 9–10

liability limits in insurance, 12–14
home businesses and, 12–13
pools and spas, 13
special needs (valuable possessions), 14

life insurance, 19
lighting, 171–175
  skylights, 170–171
loan to value (LTV), refinancing the
    mortgage and, pulling money out
    through, 28
locks s, 88–89, 127
losses, deductible status of, 71

M
maintenance, 181–191
  fall seasonal maintenance, 182–186
  spring seasonal maintenance,
    186–191
market value, 113
Microsoft Money Premium for tax
    accounting, **64**
Moving Day, 131–136
  delays in, 135–136
  DSL or cable modems hookups,
    133
  early start on, 134
  estimates of time/cost in, 135
  moving companies for, 134
  prioritizing items for, 136
  problems on, 135
  utility hookups for, 131–133,
    132–133t
  wireless networking, 133–134

N
National Association of Home
    Inspectors (NAHI), 123
neighborhood, 51
  active role in, 60
  neighborhood watch programs and,
    90
  nuisances in, 58–60
  property values climbing in, 102
  renovations and, 37–38
  security and, 86
neighborhood watch programs, 90
net value of home, 116, 117t
nonrenewal of insurance, 15–16

P
paint, 128
  maintenance of, 184, 189
permits for renovations, 42
personal property insurance, 10–11
pests, 190
  Before You Move In check of, 125
pet odors, 128
planning department, 52
plumbing systems, 175–178
  water heaters, 185–186
points on mortgage, as tax deduction,
    68–69
pool/spa, 178–180
  insurance and, 13
  maintenance of, 189–190
premium increases in insurance, 15–16
property taxes, 66–67

Q
Quicken Premier for tax accounting,
    63

R
record keeping. *See* taxes
refinancing the mortgage, 21–32
  adjustable vs. fixed rate mortgages
    and, 31–32
  capital gains taxes and, 27
  credit rating and, 23
  deductible mortgage interest and, 25
  equity needed from, 23–27
  home equity loans vs., 30
  home improvement loans vs., 30
  home improvements and, money for,
    24–25
  interest rates and, 22–23, 26
  loan to value (LTV) and pulling
    money out through, 28
  penalties for, 23
  qualifying for, 27
  second mortgages and, 28–30
  tax implications of, 25
  when to consider, 21

renovations, 137–180, 193–200
  age of home and, 39
  appreciation of value in, 35–36
  bathroom, 46–47, **47**, 195–196
  Before You Move In check of,
    129–130
  carpeting, 167–170
  ceilings, "popcorn", 137–140
  central heat/ac, 152–156
  consultants for, 41, 193
  cosmetic changes and, 49
  current value of home and, 114–116
  designers and architects for, 199–200
  do-it-yourself, 42
  doors, 145–148
  electrical systems, 175–178
  fireplace surrounds, 159–161
  fixtures, 196
  improvements vs.
    maintenance/repair and, 71
  insulation, 156–159
  Internet resources for, 197–198
  justifications for, 37
  kitchen appliances, 161–164
  kitchen, 44–46, 195–196
  lighting, 171–175
  magazines and books on, 194
  market timing and, 39–40
  motivation for, 48–49
  neighborhood and, 37–38
  overdoing it, overbuilding for
    neighborhood, 35
  permits for, 42
  planning for, 41
  plumbing systems, 175–178
  pools/spas, 178–180
  price range of house and, 38–39
  repairs vs., 40
  resale values and, 33–34, 36–37
  resources for, 193–194
  return on investment vs. market
    appreciation in, 36
  roof, 164–167
  room heaters, 149–152
  safety and, 43
  selling vs., 46

renovations (*Cont.*):
  showrooms to generate ideas for, 195
  skylights, 170–171
  tax implications of, 71
  time in residence and, 37, 48
  TV shows and, 199
  what to improve, for best resale
    value, 34, 40, 43, **48**
  window coverings, 143–145
  windows, 140–143
rental properties, taxes and, 80
repairs vs. renovations, 40
replacement costs and insurance, 8,
    17–18
roofs, 127, 164–167
  maintenance of, 184–185
room heaters, 149–152

S
safety, in renovating work, 43
Seasonal Energy Efficiency Rating
    (SEER) 154–155
seasonal maintenance, 181–191
second mortgages, 28–30
  blended interest rates in, 29
  disadvantages of, 29–30
  home equity loans vs., 30
  home improvement loans vs., 30
security, 85–99
  discouraging attempted break-ins in,
    94
  electronic security systems for, 91–95
  electronic sensors and, 89
  identify theft and, 98
  neighborhood and, 86
  neighborhood watch programs and,
    90
  physical protection for your home
    in, 86–87
  resources for, 99
  security companies and, 90–91
  surveillance systems for, 95–98
  window/door bars as, 87–88
  window/door locks as, 88–89
  X10 electronic security systems in, 93

security companies, 90–91
security systems, 91–95
selling your home, 77–84. *See also* taxes
   adjusted tax basis in, 69–70
   capital gain in, 70
   tax implications of, 69–71
skylights, 170–171
smells, 124–125
smoke detectors, fire extinguishers, 127
spring seasonal maintenance, 186–191
structural cracks, 190–191
surveillance systems, 95–98

T
tax basis, 69–70
taxes, 25, 61–75
   adjusted tax basis in, 69–70
   Alternative Minimum Tax (AMT)
      and, 68
   banks as holder of financial records
      for, 65
   capital gains. *See also* selling your
      home and capital gains, below,
      27, 70, 77
   credit cards and, 63
   deductible mortgage interest and,
      25, 67–68
   depreciation and, 70
   electronic files as records for, 66
   general receipts for, 72
   home office and, 72–74
   improvements vs.
      maintenance/repair and, 71
   losses are not deductible from, 71
   Microsoft Money Premium for tax
      accounting, **64**
   paper trails and documentation in,
      64–66
   points on mortgage as deduction in,
      68–69
   property, 66–67
   Quicken Premier for tax accounting,
      63
   recordkeeping for, 61–63
   rental properties and, 80

taxes (*Cont.*):
   selling your home and capital gains
      taxes, 69–71, 77–84
   age requirement in, 78
   employment status changes and, 82
   exceptions to rules in, 81–82
   exclusion amount in, determining, 83
   exclusion amount in, reporting, 83
   extended vacations from residence
      and, 80–81
   Form 2119 and, 79
   health crises and, 82
   move away requirement in, 79
   new rules for, 79
   once in a lifetime exclusion in, 79
   "principal residence" status in, 79–80
   recordkeeping for, 83–84
   reinvesting in property and, 78
   rental properties and, 80
   rollover in, 78
   spouse qualification and, 81
   "unforeseen events" exception and, 82
   unmarried joint owners, 81
   tax planning for, 77
   taxable items in, 66–69
   utilities and, as deductions, 72
tie downs (earthquake regions), 127
title insurance, 9–10, 114
TV shows and renovation, 199

U
umbrella insurance plans, 13
upgrading the home. *See* renovations,
   137
utilities
   Before You Move In check of,
      125–127
   hookups for, 131–133, 132–133*t*
   tax deductibility of, 72

V
valuables, insurance for, 14
variances, 52
video surveillance systems, 95–98

W

warranty plans, insurance and, 5–6
water heaters
 Before You Move In check of, 126
 maintenance of, 185–186
weather stripping, 186
window coverings, 143–145
window/door bars, 87–88
window/door locks, 88–89
windows and screens, 129, 140–143
 maintenance of, 191
 skylights, 170–171
wireless networking, 133–134
wiring, rewiring
 Before You Move In check of, 126

wiring, rewiring (*Cont.*):
 electrical systems, 175–178
wood burning stoves, 151

X

X10 electronic security systems, 93

Z

zoning, 52–55
 homeowner's associations (HOA),
  56–58
 notices of changes in, 55
 taking action against changes to, 56

About the Author

Robert Irwin is the author of McGraw-Hill's bestselling
Tips and Traps series and is one of America's leading real
estate experts. Robert Irwin's books have sold more than
one million copies.